# De Soto, Coronado, Cabrillo

## Explorers of the *Northern Mystery*

By David Lavender
Produced by the
Division of Publications
National Park Service

U.S. Department of the Interior
Washington, D.C.

*Mitzner*

*About this book*
American history begins not with the English at
Jamestown or the Pilgrims at Plymouth but with
Spanish exploration of the border country from
Florida to California in the 16th century. This handbook describes the expeditions of three intrepid
explorers—De Soto, Coronado, and Cabrillo—their
adventures, their encounters with native inhabitants,
and the consequences, good and ill, of their jour-
neys. This little-known story is related by David
Lavender, author of many books on the American
West. His work gives perspective to the several
national parks that commemorate the first Spanish
explorations.

National Park Handbooks, compact introductions to
the natural and historical places administered by the
National Park Service, are designed to promote
public understanding and enjoyment of the parks.
These handbooks are intended to be informative
reading and useful guides. More than 100 titles are in
print. They are sold at parks and by mail from the
Superintendent of Documents, U.S. Government
Printing Office, Washington, D.C. 20402.

*Library of Congress Cataloging-in-Publication Data*
Lavender, David Sievert, 1910-
De Soto, Coronado, Cabrillo: explorers of the north-
ern mystery/by David Lavender.
p.    cm.—(Handbook; 144)
    1. United States—Discovery and exploration—
Spanish. 2. Soto, Hérnando, de, ca. 1500-1542. 3. Co-
ronado, Francisco Vásques de, 1510-1554. 4. Cabrillo,
Juan Rodrígues, d. 1543. 5. Explorers—United States—
History—16th century. I. Title. II. Series: Handbook
(United States. National Park Service. Division of
Publications); 144
E123.L24    1992    973.1—dc20    91-47633
CIP 1992

# Prologue

A magic date: 1492. The year began with Christopher Columbus watching the Moors surrender the city of Granada, their last stronghold in Spain, to the joint monarchs Ferdinand and Isabella. He reminded them of the triumph in a summation he wrote later of what he too had accomplished that year. "I saw the banners of your Highnesses raised on the towers of the Alhambra in the city of Granada, and I saw the Moorish king go out of the gate of the city and kiss the hands of your Highnesses and of my lord the Prince." Shortly after the victory, he added, "your Highnesses . . . determined to send me, Christopher Columbus to the countries of India, so that I might see what they were like, the lands and the people, and might seek out and know the nature of everything that is there. . . ."

This remarkable coincidence—the expulsion of the Moors from Spain and Columbus's almost simultaneous discovery of the "Indies"—resulted in a burst of explosive expansionism. The following year, 1493, Columbus established Spain's first colony in the New World on the island of Hispaniola, occupied now by Haiti and the Dominican Republic. By 1515 Cuba had been conquered and its cities of Santiago and Havana established as bases for further exploration. In 1519 Hernán Cortés swept out of Cuba into Mexico and found a new source of wealth for his country, his followers, and himself by looting the Aztec empire of stores of gold and silver the Indians had been accumulating for centuries. A decade later Francisco Pizarro began his dogged and even more lucrative conquest of the Incas of Peru.

Meanwhile, what of the Northern Mystery, as historian Herbert E. Bolton aptly named the unknown lands above Mexico? Was it not logical that similar treasures awaited discovery there? And so the fever for adventure and riches drew three more distance-defying explorers—Hernando de Soto, Francisco Vásquez de Coronado, and Juan Rodríguez Cabrillo—into three different parts of what is now the United States. Each reached as far as he did because inside him burned the awesome, often contradictory, but always steel-bright fires of medieval Spain.

Our tangible connection to this age of pathfinding and discovery is a scattering of historic places stretching from Florida to California. They are evidence of Spanish life and color in the old borderlands. This book draws into a whole the stories of several such places. Here are the beginnings of Spanish North America.

---

*This 16th-century woodcut, the product of an artist with a fertile imagination but little information, epitomizes the contemporary view that European discoverers were bringing civilization to the grateful natives of the New World.*

# Routes of the Explorers

The first Spanish expeditions into the northern borderlands of New Spain sampled the continent's wondrous diversity. De Soto made his great march across a luxuriant country so stunning and productive that the expedition's journals are full of admiring description. He encountered complex native societies, which were often organized into powerful chiefdoms—generous in peace but formidable in war. Centuries of settlement has greatly altered this landscape. Not so Coronado's country. A traveler to the Southwest can still see places evocative of the first Spanish encounters with Indians of the pueblos and Plains. A sailor retracing Cabrillo's route up the California coast runs past mountains that, in the words of the chronicler, "seem to reach the heavens ... [and are] covered with snow"—mountains he called the Sierra Nevada. They are today's Santa Lucia range. Cabrillo's voyage is now best followed in the imagination.

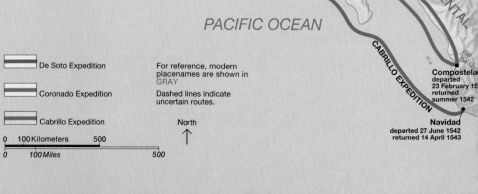

Rogue River

Cape Mendocino

Voyage continues under Ferrer after Cabrillo's death.

Point Reyes

San Francisco

Monterey Bay

SANTA LUCIA RANGE

Cabo de Galera
Point Conception

Isla Posesión
Death of Cabrillo

CHANNEL ISLANDS

Los Angeles

San Miguel
San Diego
Cabrillo National Monument

BAJA CALIFORNIA

GULF OF CALIFORNIA

CALIFORNIA

ROCKY MOUNTAINS

Colorado River

GRAND CANYON

Tusayan

Cicuyé
Pecos National Historical Park

Santa Fe
Tiquex

Háwikuh

Acoma

Phoenix

San Pedro River

CORONADO EXPEDITION

Coronado National Memorial

SIERRA MADRE OCCIDENTAL

Sonora

Hermosillo

Rio

Rio Conchos

Culiacán

SUPPLY SHIPS

PACIFIC OCEAN

CABRILLO EXPEDITION

Rio

Compostela
departed 23 February 15
returned summer 1542

Navidad
departed 27 June 1542
returned 14 April 1543

De Soto Expedition

Coronado Expedition

Cabrillo Expedition

For reference, modern placenames are shown in GRAY

Dashed lines indicate uncertain routes.

North

0  100 Kilometers  500

0  100 Miles  500

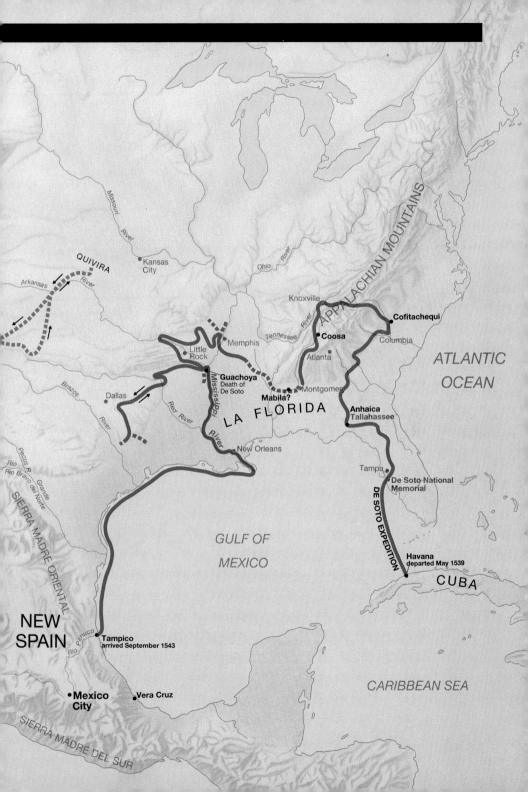

QUIVIRA

Missouri River

Kansas City

Arkansas River

Ohio River

Knoxville

APPALACHIAN MOUNTAINS

Cofitachequi

Tennessee River

Coosa

Columbia

Memphis

Little Rock

Atlanta

ATLANTIC OCEAN

Brazos River

Dallas

Guachoya
Death of De Soto

Mabila?

Montgomery

Mississippi River

Red River

LA FLORIDA

Anhaica
Tallahassee

New Orleans

Tampa

De Soto National Memorial

Pecos R.
Rio Grande
Rio Bravo del Norte

DE SOTO EXPEDITION

SIERRA MADRE ORIENTAL

GULF OF MEXICO

Havana
departed May 1539

CUBA

NEW SPAIN

Rio Panuco

Tampico
arrived September 1543

Mexico City

Vera Cruz

CARIBBEAN SEA

SIERRA MADRE DEL SUR

# Timeline

| First Expeditions North | 1539 | 1540 |
|---|---|---|
| **De Soto** | Lands in Florida in late May; marches through upper Florida; major battle at Napituca; guerilla war with Apalachees; winter camp at Anhaica (Tallahassee) | Following Indian trails, expedition swings in a wide arc through Georgia, South Carolina, North Carolina, and Alabama, encountering major chiefdoms. Bloody battle at Mabila (central Alabama) in October |
| **Coronado** | | Departs from Compostela with an army of 300 cavalry and infantry, several hundred Indian allies, friars, and a long pack train. Alarcón sails up the Gulf of California with three vessels. Expedition penetrates American Southwest, reaches Háwikuh in July; engages the Zuñi in battle; Coronado wounded. Tovar explores Hopi villages in Arizona. Alarcón reaches mouth of Colorado River. Cárdenas sights the Grand Canyon. Alvarado marches to Acoma, Pecos, and beyond. |
| **Cabrillo** | | Accompanies an exploring expedition up the northwest coast as *almirante* (second in command). Expedition abandoned after its leader is killed fighting Indians. |

| 1539-43 | 1562 | 1598 |
|---|---|---|
| De Soto expedition | French Huguenots settle in Florida | Oñate expedition into Southwest |

| 1540-42 | 1565 | 1607 |
|---|---|---|
| Coronado expedition | Menendez establishes St. Augustine | English settle at Jamestown |

| 1542-43 | 1584 | 1620 |
|---|---|---|
| Cabrillo's voyage | Ralegh plants colony on North Carolina coast | Pilgrims settle at Plymouth |

| 1541 | 1542 | 1543 |
|---|---|---|
| Winters among ancestral Chickasaw Indians of Mississippi and suffers attack by them; crosses Mississippi in May; travels in great loop through Arkansas; discovers buffalo hunters and a people who live in scattered houses and not in villages; endures severe winter at Autiamque | Reaches the rich chiefdom of Anilco; at nearby Guachoya, De Soto sends out scout parties who find nothing but wilderness; De Soto dies, is succeeded by Moscoso. After fruitless wandering in east Texas, Moscoso retraces route to Anilco | Winter camp at Aminoya on Mississippi; survivors—half the original number—build boats to float downriver; in September, they reach Pánuco River, in Mexico |
| Journeys to Quivira (Kansas). Winters at Tiguex; puts down an Indian revolt. | The army departs for home in April, arrives in Mexico City in mid-summer. Coronado reports to Viceroy Antonio de Mendoza on expedition, resumes his governorship of Nueva Galicia. Months later Coronado is tried for mismanagement of expedition but acquitted. | |
| Gathers a new exploring fleet for Mendoza. | Dispatched by Mendoza to continue exploration of the northwest. *June:* Sails from Navidad, near Colima, Mexico. *September 28:* Sights "a sheltered port and a very good one." This is San Diego Bay, which he names San Miguel. *October:* Sails through the Channel Islands, suffers fall and injury. *November:* Reaches the northernmost point of the voyage, perhaps Point Reyes, California, but turns back. | *January 3:* Dies on San Miguel Island (Channel Islands). *February:* The fleet sails north again, perhaps as far as Oregon before turning back. *April:* Fleet arrives back at Navidad, nine months after embarking. |

# The Spanish *Entradas*

# The Ways of the Conquerors

*In 1493 on his second voyage Columbus stopped at St. Croix, one of the U.S. Virgin Islands. It was then "a very beautiful and fertile" island cultivated by Carib Indians. A boat he sent ashore met with a canoe full of Caribs. In an ensuing fight, one Indian was killed and several captured — the first serious hostilities with New World natives. Salt River Bay National Historical Park preserves the scene of this fateful encounter.*

An estimated 3,000 battles wracked the Iberian Peninsula between AD 711, when Moors from Africa invaded what became Spain, and 1492, when they were finally expelled. Nor were battles against the Moors the only ones. The Christian leaders of the peninsula's several principalities fought each other and their recalcitrant nobles in a constant quest for power, until finally Ferdinand and Isabella welded together, by marriage, all the units except Portugal.

Centralization of power in the hands of national governments was one of the characteristics that marked the slow emergence in Europe of what history calls the modern world. The reasons are manifold. A central government supported by a rising middle class of merchants and bankers was able to create big armies of professional soldiers and equip them with newly introduced gunpowder, a capability quite beyond the reach of the old feudal nobles. Concurrently, the new governments consolidated economic power, partly through nationwide taxation. New industries were encouraged. Feelings of nationalism swelled; people took pride in considering themselves Spaniards rather than just Castillians.

International trade assumed new importance, especially trade with the Orient, whose extraordinary wealth had been revealed by the adventures of the Venetian family of Polo as recounted by Marco, the youngest of the group. Land caravans to the fabled East were difficult, however, and limited by interruptions and tributes imposed by Moslem middlemen. So why not travel to the Orient by water, either by circling the southern tip of Africa or sailing due west across the Atlantic?

The most logical place in Europe for starting the endeavor was the Iberian Peninsula, which dipped down toward Africa and all but closed off the western end of the Mediterranean Sea. The exploration of Africa was launched during the middle of the 15th century by Prince Henry the Navigator of tiny Portugal. His success and that of the Portuguese rulers who followed him was so astounding that Ferdinand and Isabella at last agreed to support Columbus in a competitive transatlantic attempt. The point is vital. Spain's feudal nobles probably could not have financed the expedition; the central government of newly unified Spain did.

Columbus took the risk because he believed, as had the ancient Greeks, that the circumference of the world was much smaller than it actually was. He also believed, as had Marco Polo, that Asia extended farther east than it does. When he found land at approximately the longitude that he expected to, he assumed joyfully that he was close to Cathay (China) and the islands of India. From that misapprehension comes, of course, the name West Indies for the islands of the Caribbean and Indians for their inhabitants, a term that quickly spread throughout the hemisphere.

The islands and the eastern coasts of Central America and the northwestern part of South America that he and Amerigo Vespucci (hence the name America) skirted on separate expeditions during the following decade were disappointing—no teeming cities crowned with exotic architecture, no kings and queens dressed in flowing silk and laden with precious gems, no warehouses bulging with expensive spices. To a less energetic nation than Spain, the failure of expectations might have ended further activity. But emerging Spain saw opportunities in the wilderness. Some gold could be taken from the placer mines on the island of Hispaniola. Plantations worked by enslaved Indians could be developed on Cuba and Puerto Rico. Those Indians—all Indians—had a greater attraction than just as laborers, however. Alone of all European nations, Spain was committed to incorporating the native Americans into the empire as loyal, taxpaying subjects. Priests accompanied exploring expeditions. After the *entradas* were completed, missionaries settled among the tribes and began the civilizing process, as civilization was defined by the conquerors.

The Spaniards saw themselves as particularly fitted for carrying out this God-given program. Eight centuries of war against the Moors had brought a strong sense of unity to the peninsula's extraordinary mix of bloodlines—descendants of ancient Greeks, Romans,

*Prince Henry of Portugal (1394-1460). His attempts at reaching the Indies by out-flanking Africa earned for him the title of Navigator, though he himself never went on exploring voyages. His headquarter at Sagres on the western-most promontory of Portugal was a gathering place for cosmographers, astronomers, chartmakers, and ship-builders. Their work inaugurated in the 15th century the great age of discovery that Spain continued in the next century.*

Carthegenians, and Celts as well as indigenous Iberians. Contests with Muslims and attacks on Jews through the Inquisition (Jews were also expelled from Spain in 1492) had spread a crusading religious fervor throughout the nation. Many a Spaniard felt in his bones what was in fact the truth: Spain was poised in the 16th century for a great leap forward that would, for a time, make her the dominant power in Europe. Supreme confidence generated in many Spaniards a pride that unfriendly nations such as England regarded as arrogance.

One side effect of all this was the creation of a large class of professional soldiers who scorned all other callings. Success in battle brought them a living of sorts; victors, for example, could force Muslims to work patches of ground for them. A man could become an *hidalgo*, entitled to use the word *Don* in front of his name and pass it on, generation after generation, to his sons. The first-born of these families picked up the nation's plums. They were appointed to prestigious places in the army, the church, or the royal bureaucracy. For the rest there was little but their swords and a readiness for adventure.

The New World opened new opportunities for these younger sons and their followers. They could join small private armies that went, with the monarch's permission, into the Americas to spread the gospel among the "heathens" while simultaneously looting the defeated Indians' storehouses of treasure and taking their lands. Prime examples of this grasping for treasure are furnished by some of the *conquistadores* who hailed from the harsh, barren lands of the Extremadura region of Castile—names that still ring triumphantly throughout most of the New World: Hernán Cortés, Vasco Nuñez de Balboa, the brothers Pizarro, and Hernando de Soto.

The crown gave little except permission and titles— *adelantado* ("he who leads the way") and governor— to men such as these. But if the risks were great, so too at times were the rewards. As already indicated, there might be riches to divide after the king had taken his 20 percent share. There were plantations to be founded and tended by Indians who gave their labor, however willingly, in exchange for being taught the ways of Christians. The size of each man's share in these gains depended partly on his initial investment in the expedition. Money wasn't all. The con-

*Christopher Columbus, whose 1492 voyage opened a new world to Europeans. Though many artists have attempted portraits of Columbus, none were from life. This portrait is a copy of a painting done in 1525. After the First Voyage, the Spanish monarchs granted to Columbus and his descendents the above coat of arms. It signified his new place in the nobility. The gold castle and purple lion linked him to the sovereigns. The golden islands in the sea proclaimed his discoveries. The anchors were emblems of his rank as admiral.*

tribution could be—and this was a crucial point—energy, ability, intense patriotism, religious zeal, and often ruthlessness.

Each man took with him to the New World what he had. Apparently there were few full suits of armor, though Francisco Vásquez de Coronado did possess one that was handsomely gilded to look like the gold he was searching for.

Partial suits—coats of mail made of small, interlinked rings of metal or cuirasses of plate armor that protected the wearer's front and sides—were more numerous. Most cuirasses were made with a ridge running down the front and curved in such a way that a lance point striking the metal would, it was hoped, glance off without penetrating. It was hoped, too, that arrows would be similarly deflected. The chronicles tell, however, of Indian bows driving arrows entirely through plate armor and of cane arrows splintering on striking chain mail. The needle-sharp pieces then passed through the metal rings, inflicting puncture wounds that festered. Jackets made of quilted padding or even of tough bullhide were probably as effective against arrows as metal.

Footmen, who constituted the greater part of every New World expedition, carried pikes or halberds, crossbows or arquebuses, and sometimes maces or battle axes. A crossbow, whose string was pulled tight by a crank, propelled iron darts with great force and accuracy from grooves in the weapon's stock. An arquebus was a primitive musket about 3 feet in length but lacked accuracy at distances greater than 75 yards or so. Indians, it turned out, could shoot several arrows in the time the handler of a crossbow or arquebus could fire once.

Cavalrymen, the elite of the force, were armed with lances, swords for slashing, and daggers. Long lances were generally couched against the rider's body, as in tournaments or charges against similarly equipped European adversaries. A lance driven through an Indian's body, however, would sometimes hang up and pull the rider from his saddle. Accordingly, shorter weapons held in an upraised hand were preferred in the New World. They could be hurled or held and directed at the enemy's face—an enemy on foot, for the native Americans did not yet have horses.

The *conquistadores* were as superb horsemen as the world has seen. Their animals were loved and

*Priests accompanied most expeditions of discovery. Like their countrymen, most clergy were poorly equipped to understand and tolerate the new societies they encountered in America. One clergyman who rose far above his time and place was Bartolomé de las Casas, who spoke out against abuse of the Indians but met with great opposition from vested interests.*

pampered. During the early years in the Americas they were relatively rare and expensive (few survived the tempestuous sea journey from Europe to become breeding stock), and just the sight of them terrified Indians. The fearful impact of a cavalry charge, lances flying or thrusting, swords slashing, and wardogs sometimes racing beside the horses, goes far to explain how small groups of Spaniards were able to triumph over great numerical odds. Pedro de Casteñada, one of the historians of the Coronado expedition, put it thus: "after God, we owed the victory to the horses."

Desperation also played a part. The adventurers often found themselves hundreds of miles from any possibility of help. Stamina in the face of hunger and hardship, courage and energy in opposition to attack and fear were the basic elements of salvation. Of necessity the men adopted whatever methods promised to carry them to their goals. Religious fanaticism was another motive. To Cortés's men, the Aztecs, who regularly offered human sacrifices to a heathen god, were an abomination and deserved to be annihilated, or at least enslaved, if they did not accept the Christian salvation held out to them. This attitude carried over, in somewhat lesser degree, to all Indians, even though Spain's rulers constantly exhorted gentleness, and missionaries went with every major group to offer heaven to souls lost in darkness. That is, if Indians had souls, which many Europeans of the time sincerely doubted.

Finally, every *conquistador* was stirred to action by his own credulity. The Church had brought him up to believe implicitly in miracles. A large part of his education consisted of peopling the unknown world with marvels and monsters. A favorite tale, though by no means the only one, dealt with seven Catholic bishops and their congregations who fled from the invading Moors to the island of Antilia. There they burned their ships and diligently built seven glorious cities, for naturally Christian settlements would be more dazzling than pagan ones. *Mas allá*: there is more beyond. A wondrous dream, Spanish-style. It carried, in succession, Pánfilo Narváez, Hernando de Soto, Francisco Vásquez de Coronado, and Juan Rodríguez Cabrillo into what became the United States. There reality at last took command.

## Los Conquistadores

With a few thousand soldiers Spain conquered the Americas. Most of the soldiers were unemployed veterans of an army tempered by long compaigns against the Moors in Iberia and the French in North Italy. They came to America, wrote an eyewitness, "to serve God and His Majesty, to give light to those who were in darkness, and to grow rich, as all men desire to do."

*Los conquistadores* were tough, disciplined, and as ruthless as circumstances required. Their weapons— evolved in the formal battle of Europe—were the matchlock musket (sometimes called an arquebus), the crossbow, pikes, lances (carried by cavalry), swords, cannon, and above all the horse, which Indians universally regarded as a supernatural being. This weaponry served well against organized armies in Central Amer-

Cavalryman in armor

Pikeman

*Arquebusier, c. 1540*

*Crossbowman arming his weapon*

18

ica and Peru that fought in formations mostly with clubs, spears, and slings. But in North America, the Spaniards faced skilled and elusive archers who could drive an arrow through armor. The crossbow and musket soon proved useless. Far more effective were sword-wielding cavalry and infantry and (for De Soto) wardogs. In the one battle Southeast Indians had a chance of winning (Mabila, 18 October 1540), De Soto against great odds slaughtered his antagonists. Thousands died against only 18 or so Spaniards. Foreshadowing things to come, this battle demonstrated that Indians fighting with Stone Age weapons were no match against European arms and tactics.

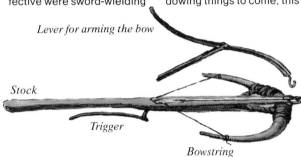

*Lever for arming the bow*

*Stock*

*Trigger*

*Bowstring*

*An infantryman armed his crossbow by pushing the bowspring back with a lever, engaging the trigger catch, and inserting a metal-tipped dart. This weapon was effective in Europe against formations and armor but less useful against a foe who quite sensibly soon learned to fight by stealth and avoid open combat.*

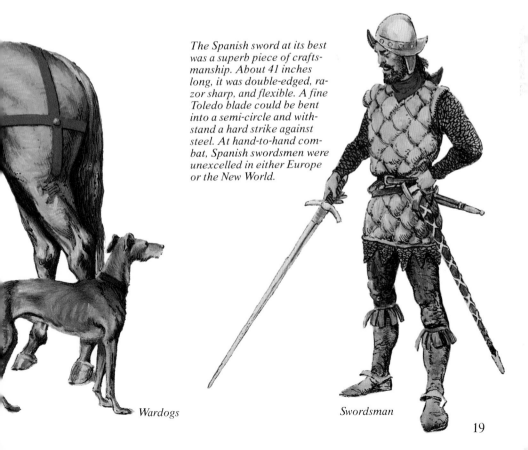

*The Spanish sword at its best was a superb piece of craftsmanship. About 41 inches long, it was double-edged, razor sharp, and flexible. A fine Toledo blade could be bent into a semi-circle and withstand a hard strike against steel. At hand-to-hand combat, Spanish swordsmen were unexcelled in either Europe or the New World.*

*Wardogs*

*Swordsman*

19

# The Wanderers

Redheaded Alvar Nuñez Cabeza de Vaca—Cabeza de Vaca translates as Cow's Head—was a man of considerable pride and, apparently, some wry humor. In 1483, about three years after his birth, its exact date unknown, his paternal grandfather, Pedro de Vera, conquered the Grand Canary Island off the northwest coast of Africa for Spain, a feat that brought a glow, in court circles, to the name de Vera. And then there was his mother's name, Teresa Cabeza de Vaca. Legend avers that back in 1212 her ancestor, a shepherd, had used the skull of a cow to mark a mountain pass that let a Christian army surprise and defeat its Mohammedan enemy. The shepherd's sovereign thereupon bestowed the name Cabeza de Vaca on the family. Young Alvar Nuñez must have enjoyed the story, for he adopted his mother's surname rather than his father's, a not unusual custom in Spain.

He fought in several battles for Ferdinand and Isabella and for their grandson, Charles V, and was severely wounded at least once. In 1526, when he was about 46, Charles appointed him royal treasurer of a large expedition Pánfilo de Narváez proposed to lead into Florida, a name that then covered a huge region stretching from the peninsula around the dimly known north Gulf Coast to the Río de las Palmas in northeastern Mexico.* If treasure was found—and treasure was Narváez's goal—it would be up to Cabeza de Vaca to make sure the king received his 20 percent share. Other financial duties were involved, so that altogether it seemed a promising appointment for a middle-aged ex-soldier and able administrator. As events turned out, Vaca could hardly have suffered a greater misfortune.

The problem, which merits a digression, was Pánfilo de Narváez, the expedition's leader. About the same age as Cabeza de Vaca, he was tall, courtly, and deep voiced, qualities that helped marvelously in advancing his career. He had prospered as a pioneer settler in Jamaica, and between 1511 and 1515 had aided

*Paul Horgan in *Great River* identifies Rio de las Palmas with today's Rio Grande. Other historians favor Soto la Marina, about 30 miles north of Tampico, formerly Pánuco.

Diego Velásquez in the conquest of Cuba, a feat which had elevated Velásquez to the governorship of the island. Both men added to their riches by using enforced Indian labor to exploit the island's shallow placer mines and embryonic plantations. And although both could easily have retired to comfortable estates, each wanted more money, a common itch.

As chief administrator of Cuba, Velásquez was allowed by the government in Spain to authorize explorations of the Caribbean. In 1517 and 1518 he exercised this right by licensing seafarers to explore and trade along the coasts of Yucatan and Mexico, capture Indian slaves, and scout out the country for booty. In return for the licenses, Velásquez would share in whatever gains resulted.

Of his searchers for new wealth, the one whose name would ring down through history was Hernán Cortés. Cocky, crafty, reckless, and adept with the ladies, Cortés had come to Cuba as Velásquez's private secretary at the same time Narváez had. He, too, had prospered, but unlike Narváez he had quarreled sharply with his former boss. Though a reconciliation had been effected, it was touchy. Still, Cortés had money and was willing to spend it on risky adventures, and so, in 1518, he was authorized to explore Mexico's eastern coast. He assembled a fleet of 11 ships, 16 precious horses, and prodigious stores of armaments. People grew so excited about his prospects that he easily recruited 500 or so soldiers and 100 sailors—nearly half of Cuba's male population.

While he was preparing his expedition, some of Velásquez's other scouts returned with rumors of a fabulous empire of Aztec Indians and their capital city, Tenochtitlán, built on an island in a shallow lake that filled most of a high mountain valley in Mexico. Growing suddenly nervous about Cortés—how loyal would he be with treasure in front of him and an army at his back?—Velásquez in February 1519 revoked Cortés's commission. Defying him, Cortés slipped away and disappeared.

One of the world's most fabulous adventures followed. Landing on the Yucatan coast, Cortés rescued a survivor of one of Velásquez's earlier expeditions—a man who in his captivity had learned the Mayan language. Employing the one-time prisoner as an interpreter, Cortés turned his fleet northward, probing the coast. Such resistance as developed among the

*Charles, King of Spain, 1516-56, and Emperor of the Holy Roman Empire, 1519-58. Under his rule, Spain carved out a new empire in the Americas to go with its dominions in Europe.*

Indians was quickly crushed by the terrifying aspect of the expedition's few horses. During one of those aborted battles, Cortés rescued yet another captive, a woman named Malinche whom the priest with the expedition baptized and named Marina.

Marina was a Nahua, or Aztec. While in captivity she too had learned the Mayan tongue and could converse with the rescued Spaniard. Through this linguistic conduit, the *conquistadores* received exciting information about Tenochtitlán, the glittering city of the Aztecs, predecessor of today's Mexico City. A dazzling prize! And why, Cortés surely wondered, should he share any of it with Diego Velásquez, sitting safely at home in Cuba?

On April 21, 1519, the fleet dropped anchor at the sea end of a trail leading to the city. There Cortés laid the foundations of a port that he named Vera Cruz (today Veracruz). Calling his men together—they, too, were excited about prospects—he prevailed on the majority to elect him captain-general of the expedition, a move that in Cortés's mind freed him of his obligations to Velásquez and made him answerable only to King Charles V. Simultaneously, he sent emissaries to Moctezuma, emperor of the Aztecs, asking for an audience.

The timing could hardly have been more propitious. The Aztec rule was harsh; subject nations seethed with discontent; Tenochtitlán itself was torn with dissensions. Fearful that the strangers might be able to capitalize on the undercurrents of the rebellion—and fearful, too, that the newcomers might somehow be descendants of the ancient serpent-god, Quetzalcoatl—Moctezuma tried to buy off the Spaniards. Down to Veracruz went five noble diplomats accompanied by 100 porters laden with treasure. All of it was breathtaking, but what really dumbfounded the Spaniards were two metal disks the size of cartwheels. One, representing the Sun God, was of solid gold. The other, dedicated to the Moon, was of silver.

Cortés declined to respond as expected. He loaded the treasure onto one of his ships and ordered the captain to sail directly to Spain, where he would use the booty to win the approval of Charles V. The rest of the ships he burned so that none of the men in the command who were still loyal to Velásquez could return to Cuba and stir up trouble there. As for his own men, they too would fight harder if they knew

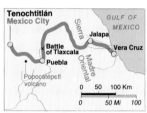

*Hernán Cortés with 600 men and 16 horses overthrew the Aztec empire. This illustration of the conquistador was made from life. The map traces his route from the coast to Tenochtitlán in 1519.*

that no ships were waiting to evacuate them if they were defeated.

In November 1519, Tenochtitlán capitulated after a short, hard fight. Cortés took Moctezuma hostage and then paused to contemplate his enormous prize.

Unknown to the victors, the captain of the ship bound for Spain did pause in Cuba to check on some land he owned there. It was a short stay but long enough for the sailors to talk. Astounded couriers sped the word to Velásquez. The governor was outraged. He was already at work gathering a strong force of 900 men equipped with 80 horses and 13 ships to pursue Cortés and arrest him for defying orders. Doubly furious at what seemed to him Cortés's latest treachery, he put Pánfilo de Nárvaez in charge of a punitive force to bring the disloyal *conquistador* back to Cuba in chains!

Warnings from Veracruz reached Cortés at the Aztec capital. He reacted with characteristic boldness. Leaving two hundred men at Tenochtitlán, he marched the rest swiftly to the coast. No one there anticipated him so soon. Late at night, when most of his would-be captors were asleep, he waded his men across a swollen stream and attacked without warning. During the chaos that followed, a lance point put out one of Nárvaez's eyes. By dawn the field was in Cortés's hands. Most of Nárvaez's men, hearing of the riches of Tenochtitlán, deserted their commander and swore fealty to the victor.

While Nárvaez remained under guard at Veracruz, nursing his wound, Cortés marched back to rejoin the rest of his men at Tenochtitlán. The Aztecs let the returning soldiers reach the palace compound and then attacked in waves of thousands. The hostage emperor, Moctezuma, was stoned to death by his own people while pleading for peace. Trying once again to use the night as cover, Cortés on June 30, 1520, led hundreds of Spaniards and several thousand Indian allies onto one of the stone-and-earth causeways that connected the island city to the mainland. Aztecs swarmed after them in canoes. On that famed *noche triste*—night of sorrows—850 Spaniards and upwards of 4,000 of their allies died.

Fortune shifted quickly, however. Wheeling around on the plains outside the city and making adroit use of his few horses and guns, Cortés defeated the army pursuing him. Doggedly then he put together a fresh

*Xipe Totec, Aztec god of fertility, one of many gods in the Aztec pantheon, redrawn from the original codex. He wears the flayed skin of a sacrificial victim. Ritual killing horrified Spaniards and in their eyes justified the conquest. But to Aztecs the gods and their extravagent costumes were an important part of everyday life, condensations of vital social truths.*

army of Indians who hated the Aztecs and of whites who were dribbling into Mexico to see what was going on. The next year, on August 13, 1521, he recaptured Tenochtitlán, again at heavy cost. By twisting logic only a little, he could have blamed all these troubles on Narváez's inept interference. He did not. He treated the man kindly and then sent him home to Spain with, so it is said, a bagful of golden artifacts.

In Spain Narváez intrigued against the nation's hero, as Cortés then was, as best he could. He also yearned for a conquest in which he could redeem himself. When the governorship of Florida fell open, he applied for the position and won. His plan was to establish his first colony at Río de las Palmas, north of Pánuco, on Mexico's northeast coast, where Cortés had already placed a defensive outpost. From there he could put pressure on his enemy, who many of the king's council thought was growing too big for his boots. He could also search for the treasure that he was sure lay somewhere in the north, in the land from which he supposed the Aztecs had originally come—land where the fabled Seven Cities might lie.

Six hundred soldiers, sailors, and would-be settlers, a few of whom had their wives with them, left Spain aboard five ships in June 1527. One of the adventurers was Alvar Nuñez Cabeza de Vaca, making his first trip to the New World. It was a hard journey— desertions, groundings, a deadly hurricane, and finally a series of adverse storms that drove the little fleet off its intended course for the Río de las Palmas to a landing on the west coast of the Florida peninsula, probably opposite the head of Tampa Bay.

In view of the peninsula's nearness to Cuba, remarkably little was known about it. Beginning with Alonso Alvarez de Pineda in 1519, a few sea explorers had groped along its western coast on their way to Mexico. Occasional traders and slave hunters had poked into some of its lovely bays—and had often taken severe trouncings from the Indians for their pains. Juan Ponce de León, the only man to try to establish a colony there, was mortally wounded during the attempt.

Narváez must have known of the dangers, but when he saw a yellow object among some fish nets in a village from which the Indians had fled on his approach, he jumped to the conclusion that it was gold. Hopefully, he showed the object to some Indians he

"I saw the things which have been brought to the King from the new land of gold, a sun all of gold a whole fathom broad, and a moon all of silver of the same size, also two rooms full of the armour of the people there, and all manner of wondrous weapons of [the Aztecs], harnesses and darts, very strange clothing, beds and all kinds of wonderful objects of human use, much better worth of seeing than prodigies. These things are so precious that they are valued at a hundred thousand florins. All the days of my life I have seen nothing that rejoiced my heart so much as these things, for I saw among them wonderful works of art, and I marvelled at the subtle *ingenia* of people in foreign lands. Indeed, I cannot express all that I thought there."
—*Albrecht Dürer upon seeing the Aztec objects Cortés sent Charles V in 1519.*

# Tenochtitlán, Capital of the Aztec Empire

Tenochtitlán, predecessor of today's Mexico City, was one of the most magnificent cities in the world when Cortés and his small army arrived in 1519. The sight of the radiant city in the center of a large lake astonished the Spaniards. "We did not know what to say, or whether what appeared before us was real," wrote a soldier, "for there were great cities along the shore and many others in the lake, all filled with canoes, and at intervals along the causeways there were many bridges. . . ."

About 250,000, persons lived here and in its sister city Tlatelolco (left). The market place was huge. "Some of the soldiers with us had been in many parts of the world, in Constantinople and all over Italy and Rome, and they said they had never seen a public square so perfectly laid out, so large, so orderly, and so full of people."

At the center of the city—and the Aztec religion—was the *Templo Major*, a complex of temples with shrines to the gods of fertility and war—the sources of Aztec power.

The surfaces of the temples were richly ornamented in symbols and myths that expressed their complete vision of life. It was this city, which governed a vast empire in central Mexico, that the intrepid Cortés and his band overthrew in 1521.

Within a few years a splendid and original civilization lay in ruins.

lured into camp, they pointed north and said vehemently, "Apalachee! Apalachee!" Straightway Narváez decided to march there overland with the main part of his force, 40 of them mounted on the skin-and-bone horses that had survived the sea journey. The rest of the group, including its women, were directed to sail along the coast to a harbor supposedly known to the expedition's pilot. There the two groups would come together again.

Cabeza de Vaca protested. They couldn't be sure they understood the Indians properly. Would the two parties be able to find each other again on the intricate coast? They did not have food enough for exploring. First they should locate their colony in an area suitable for farming and send the ships to Cuba for supplies. Time enough then to search for gold.

Narváez waved him aside. The ships sailed on and the land party headed north, each man carrying two pounds of biscuits and half a pound of bacon. After 15 days of hunger they luckily seized some Indians who led them to a field of maize ripe enough for harvesting. Strengthened somewhat but beset by clouds of insects, they waded on through bogs, built rafts for crossing rivers—a drowned horse fed some of them one night—and then entered a region of enormous trees where piles of fallen timber created an almost impassable maze.

Apalachee, located close to the site of modern Tallahassee, turned out to be a village of 40 small houses roofed with thatch. No gold. Disgruntled, Narváez imprisoned an Apalachee chief and appropriated some of the houses for shelter. The villagers retaliated by setting fire to the buildings, a tactic that became common during later years.

The invaders stayed 25 days, scouting the surrounding country and resting as best they could under constant sniping by displaced inhabitants. They then headed west toward another town of reputed richness, Aute, near present-day St. Marks, on Apalachee Bay. Indians shadowed them, killing or wounding several men with hard-pointed arrows capable of piercing armor. Cabeza de Vaca was one of those nicked.

On the Spaniards' approach, the inhabitants of Aute burned their huts and fled. There was no gold in the ruins. No silver. No jewels. And no sign of Spanish ships in the bay. As a mysterious fever began felling the men one by one, Narváez said that Pánuco

*The Aztecs and kindred people were wonderful artists in gold. The lifesize breastplate is Mixtecan, perhaps the representation of the god of death. The gold plug below is an Aztecan facial ornament. Nobles and military leaders routinely wore plugs as a sign of rank. The plugs were inserted through a hole below the lip or in the cheek.*

could not be far away. If they could build boats . . .

How? The men knew nothing about the art of ship-building. The only materials they had were what they and their horses wore. Total helplessness—until God's will, Cabeza de Vaca wrote years later, prompted one anonymous fellow to say he thought he could make a bellows out of deerskin and wooden pipes. With the bellows they could produce heat enough to transform spurs, bridle-bits, crossbow darts, and iron stirrups into nails. Excited by that proposal, a Greek spoke up, saying he knew how to manufacture water-proofing pitch from the resin in the pine trees surrounding them.

Working with the energy of desperation, the men put together, between August 5 and September 20 five crude boats, each about 33 feet long. They made sails out of their clothing, rope out of horse hair and palmetto fibre, anchors out of stone. Those not involved in the construction used the surviving horses— a diminishing number since they killed one every third day for food—to bring in 640 bushels of corn from the fields at Aute. Several men died from fever or wounds received from the Indians—not altogether an ill wind, since the five boats could not have carried more than the 250 or so persons who overloaded them at sailing time. Narváez, exercising a leader's prerogative, picked out the best boat and strongest crew for himself.

They crawled along close to the shore, sat out storms behind islands, lost more men to Indian attack, and suffered so terribly from thirst—the water bottles they had made from horsehide soon rotted— that four of them drank salt water in their misery and perished. A more historic moment than any of them would ever realize came toward the end of October 1528, when, as they were edging out past some marshy islands, a powerful current of fresh water swept them far out to sea. They had discovered the mouth of a great river—the Mississippi.

As they worked back toward the coast on the far side of the river mouth, winds and sea currents quickened their pace. Despite strenuous efforts the crews could not keep the boats together. The men with Cabeza de Vaca grew so exhausted that they shouted to Narváez to toss them a rope and help pull them along. Narváez refused. "When the sun sank," the treasurer recalled later, "all who were in my boat were fallen one on another, so near to death that there were few of them in a state of sensibility." They lay inert throughout the night. At dawn—it was November 6, 1528—Cabeza de Vaca heard the tumult of breakers but could take no measures to meet the threat. A giant wave lifted the boat out of the water and dropped it with a crash on what was either Galveston Island off the coast of Texas or a nearby stub of a peninsula.

Karankawa Indians who had gathered at the spot to dig roots succored them. A little later they joined the crew of another capsized boat that had been commanded by captains Alonso de Castillo and Andrés Dorantes, whose black slave Estéban was with him. The combined group numbered about 80, most of them infirm and next to naked. Numbly, they tried to repair Cabeza de Vaca's boat so the strongest could sail to Pánuco for help. It sank. Four volunteers then agreed to try to reach Mexico by land. They never returned.

A winter of intense cold, starvation, and fever left only 15 alive, Cabeza de Vaca barely so. In the spring, 13 of the survivors moved off with the greater part of the Indians in search of food, leaving Cabeza de Vaca and a second invalid, Lope de Oviedo, behind with a small band. As soon as Cabeza de Vaca was able to work, the Indians set him to digging roots and carrying firewood. To escape the drudgery he became a trader, traveling far inland with a pack of shells, flints, cane for arrow shafts, sinews and so on for barter. During the wanderings he became the first European known to have seen bison.

His great desire was to walk southwest along the coast until he reached other men of his own kind, and he urged Oviedo to join him. The fellow kept promising he would as soon as he was better. Not wishing to desert a fellow Spaniard, Cabeza de Vaca wasted four years through one postponement after another. At last they started, but then Oviedo caved in with fear and turned back, preferring familiar miseries to the unknown.

Shortly thereafter, in 1532, in the bottomlands of the Colorado River of Texas, where several bands were harvesting walnuts, Cabeza de Vaca stumbled joyously across Castillo, Dorantes, and the vigorous black Esteban. The trio were also ready to strike for Mexico if they could escape from their

*The "hunch-backed cows" that Vaca and his companions saw were the wide-ranging American bison. "They have small horns like the cows of Morocco," he wrote. "The hair is very long and wooly like a rug. Some are tawny, others are black. In my judgment the flesh is finer and fatter than cows from [Spain]."*

masters, but they warned against fierce tribes to the southwest. They should try a route farther north.

After two years of interruption and frustrations they made the break. The incredible journey, broken by long stays at various Indian camps, lasted two years. At times they traveled alone. More often they were accompanied by Indians. After they had chanced to pray over an ailing man, who thereupon leaped up and declared himself cured, they became revered as supernatural medicinemen, children of the sun. Their marches, often scouted out for them by Estéban, who also served as interpreter—he learned six languages during those arduous years—became triumphal processions. Sometimes, says Cabeza de Vaca, as many as 4,000 Indians would accompany them from one village to the next, a figure that, as Bernard DeVoto has pointed out, should be taken as a way of saying "quite a few." Those who escorted them would often loot the first village they reached, whereupon its inhabitants, moving on with the quartet to another village, would recoup their losses by plundering it.

What route did they follow? No one knows. Cabeza de Vaca's descriptions of Indian customs, rivers, mountains, vegetation, and so on have led some students to suggest that the wanderers may have gone as far north as southern New Mexico and Arizona. Others think they traveled out of west Texas into Chihuahua. But whatever the way, it eventually merged with one of the trade trails that ran between the Pueblo Indian towns of the Southwest and those in the heavily populated, southward trending valleys of Sonora. They reached the Sonora area in the spring of 1536.

What had they seen along the way? Not much, according to a report that the survivors sent to the *audiencia* in Hispaniola in 1537. Just buffalo robes that had originated in the country of the plains Indians and beautifully woven cotton mantas that their native hosts had obtained by trade with Indians somewhere in the north (probably the Pueblos of the Rio Grande). Bits of coral and turquoise. And miles and miles of desolation, thinly populated by primitive tribes. Writing a memoir of the trip six years later, Cabeza de Vaca improved only slightly on the tales. In Sonora, he related, he was given five emeralds shaped like arrowheads; the donors said the "jewels" had been purchased in the north with parrot feathers and plumes. Sadly, he lost the five artifacts before anyone else saw them. He also told of handling a small bell made of copper and of hearing stories about large cities filled with big houses and surrounded by boundless fields of maize.

Such reports were too vague and understated to create much popular excitement—at first. But as Antonio de Mendoza, New Spain's first and recently arrived viceroy, realized, the calm might not last. For a similar story told a few years earlier to the infamous Nuño de Guzmán by an Indian slave named Tejo had stirred up a violent reaction.

At the time Guzmán had been governor of Pánuco on Mexico's northeast coast and was making a fortune selling slaves to plantations throughout the West Indies. But that wasn't enough, and his ears pricked up when he listened to Tejo telling about a trip with his father to seven marvelous cities far to the northwest—cities whose streets were lined with the shops of goldsmiths and silversmiths.

The story may well have had an element of truth in it. If a trader kept traveling northwest from Pánuco—and some of Mexico's early Indian traders were far-ranging—he would eventually reach the impressive pueblo towns of today's New Mexico. Where the notion of goldsmiths came from is something else, but Guzmán believed it because he wanted to.

Instead of taking a direct line to his goal, he put together a strong force, fought his way across the mountains to the west coast, and hewed out, as a base of operations for a thrust along the trade trails leading north, the all-but-independent province of Nueva Galicia. (It embraced the better part of the present-day Mexican states of Nayarit and Sinaloa.) Illness and then his arrest for his slave-dealings put a stop to the northern plans, but the appearance of the Vaca party out of the wilderness might, Mendoza feared, lead the great Cortés to appropriate the idea for himself.

Cortés was ripe for trouble. Because of his insubordination to Diego Velásquez of Cuba, the king had refused to name him viceroy of New Spain, but then had tried to compensate for the injustice, as Cortés considered it, by naming him the Marquís of the Valley of Oaxaca and giving him the right to explore the South Seas (south of Asia) for new principalities. On their quests some of his ship captains stirred Guzmán's jealousy by sailing north along the coast of Nueva Galicia. When Guzmán seized one of those ships in the port of Chiametla, the Marquís rushed up with a small army and took it back. He then used that ship to cross what he called the Sea of Cortés (today's Gulf of California) and claim possession, in the name of the king, of pearl fisheries his mariners had discovered at La Paz in what we call Baja California. The fisheries were not proving lucrative, however, and the least sign that something better existed farther north might tempt him to push on.

It behooved Mendoza, as the king's representative, to move first, before New Spain's legitimate northward expansion was halted by one of these semi-autonomous *conquistadores*. Dutifully reporting each of his moves to Charles V—caution was part of his nature—he asked, in turn, Castillo, Dorantes, and Cabeza de Vaca to lead a small exploring party into the north and learn what was really there. Not surprisingly, in view of their experiences, each refused.

In 1537, Cabeza de Vaca returned to Spain. Skeptics say he wanted to persuade the king to appoint him *adelantado* of Florida so that he could move independently into the north from that direction. On reaching Madrid, however, he found that Charles had already given the post to Hernando de Soto.

Years later one of De Soto's Portuguese officers from the town of Elvas—he identified himself only as a *hidalgo* (gentleman) of Spain—wrote that De Soto offered to take Cabeza de Vaca along as second in command for the sake of his guidance. Again the wanderer declined. But, said the *hidalgo*, whose accuracy cannot be checked, Vaca did drop hints to his friends and relatives that led them to sell everything they had in order to buy enough equipment to join the expedition. Possibly. But all we really know is that Cabeza de Vaca, the only man to brush against both of the *entradas* that gave the world its first views of what became the United States, never returned there himself. He was sent to South America instead.

Mendoza of course learned by ship of De Soto's appointment and of necessity had to assume that one of the new *adelantado*'s goals would be the Seven Cities. So now he had twin worries, Cortés in the west, De Soto in the east. But before considering the steps he took to checkmate them, it is well to look at De Soto's adventure, for he is the one who, through sheer luck, had the head start.

# The Odyssey of Cabeza de Vaca

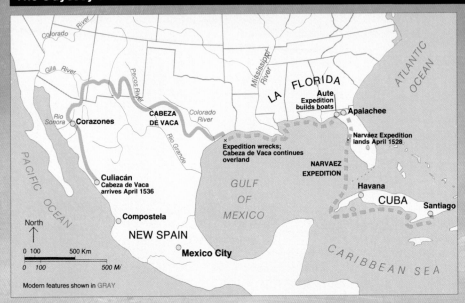

Colorado River

Gila River

Rio Sonora

**Corazones**

**CABEZA DE VACA**

Pecos River

Colorado River

Rio Grande

Mississippi River

**LA FLORIDA**

**Aute** Expedition builds boats

**Apalachee**

× Expedition wrecks; Cabeza de Vaca continues overland

Narváez Expedition lands April 1528

**NARVAEZ EXPEDITION**

ATLANTIC OCEAN

PACIFIC OCEAN

**Culiacán** Cabeza de Vaca arrives April 1536

**Compostela**

**NEW SPAIN**

GULF OF MEXICO

Havana

**CUBA**

**Santiago**

North

0 100    500 Km
0 100    500 Mi

**Mexico City**

CARIBBEAN SEA

Modern features shown in GRAY

Cabeza de Vaca and three companions, sole survivors of the ill-fated Narváez expedition (1527), were the first Europeans to cross the North American continent. They spent 8 years traveling 6,000 miles through the interior of Florida, Texas, New Mexico, Arizona, and northern Mexico. The journey itself was an incredible feat of human stamina and pluck. Equally remarkable is Cabeza De Vaca's account of his adventure. *La Relación*, first published in 1542, revised Spanish conceptions about the size and nature of the continent north of Mexico. The book is also the first detailed description of native Americans. In his wanderings Cabeza de Vaca came to admire Indians, whom he came to see as fellow humans who could be won over only by kindness. His book—which can be considered the beginning of American literature—is a record of both a physical and a spiritual journey.

# Journey into Darkness

When Hernando de Soto returned to Spain from two decades of adventure in the New World, he must have seemed to those who encountered him, or even heard of him, the embodiment of what a *conquistador* should be. He carried his tall, hard, handsome body with the unmistakable air of triumph that comes from having won by his own efforts wealth, fame, and a noble bride—all before he was 35 years old. The exact date of his birth is unknown, but it may have coincided with the last year of the 15th century. His birthplace was in the austere province of Extremadura. His father was a Méndez, his mother a de Soto; his elder brother Juan followed the Spanish custom of using both names: Juan Méndez de Soto. Hernando, the second son, chose to be different. According to his biographer, Miguel Albornoz, he was his mother's favorite. He therefore dropped Méndez from his name and became known to history only as De Soto—an appellation he carried far.

Another native of Extremadura and a neighbor of the De Soto family was Vasco Nuñez de Balboa, the fabled conqueror of Darién (Panama) and discoverer of the Pacific Ocean. Determined to emulate Balboa, who was still alive somewhere in the New World, young Hernando de Soto made his way, aged 14 or so, to Seville. There he found employment as a page in the household of the notorious schemer, 75-year-old Pedro Arias Dávila, better known as Pedrárias. When Pedrárias sailed to Central America in 1514 as a colonial administrator, De Soto went along.

He witnessed the quarrel that sprang up between his patron and Balboa, a quarrel that ended in 1519 when Balboa was convicted of treason through the intrigues of Pedrárias and beheaded. Grieving, De Soto retrieved the headless corpse and with the help of an Indian girl gave it a Christian burial. Yet he remained loyal to Pedrárias and followed him to Nicaragua, where he developed the ice-hard maturity that marked his later career. He mastered the arts of dealing in Indian slaves, looting temples, and ransacking Indian graves for valuable mortuary offerings. By such means he prospered so well that when Pizarro, also a native of Extremadura, needed help on his expedition to Peru, De Soto was able to respond with two ships and 200 men.

In the final assault on the Incas, De Soto was generally the one chosen to lead reconnoitering or vanguard parties over the difficult trails of the Andes. After the first great victory was achieved, he saw a sight that ever afterwards burned in his memory. The conquered emperor, Atahualpa (actually one of two brothers contending for the throne), offered, as his ransom, to pile a room 17 feet wide, 22 feet long, and 9 high with golden ornaments, vases, goblets, statuettes. In addition he said, he would fill a somewhat smaller adjoining chamber twice over with silver. In spite of that tremendous gesture, he was then tricked into ordering the death of his brother, for which he himself was executed. The treachery drew angry protests from De Soto.

The next conquest was of mountain-perched Cuzco, less rewarding than anticipated because it had been stripped of treasure during the filling of the rooms. Though De Soto was named lieutenant-governor, the quarrels that broke out between the generals led him to give up the position and return to Spain with his share of the booty. Various estimates of its size have been given, but since there is no satisfactory way of comparing purchasing power then and now, the figures are elusive. Still, it must have been the equivalent of several million of today's dollars.

He made a point of cutting a fine figure in Spain. Everywhere he went he was accompanied by a dazzling entourage composed mostly of officers who had ridden with him in Panama and Peru. He became a favorite of the King, to whom he loaned money; and he married a daughter of his old patron, Pedrárias. A plush life. But as the lazy days drifted by, De Soto grew restless. He needed activity and he wanted gold. Roomfuls of gold. And fame.

Yielding to his importunities, Charles V made him governor of Cuba and *adelantado* of Florida, which then stretched from the Atlantic as far north as the Carolinas and on around the Gulf of Mexico to the Río de las Palmas. The usual stipulations about the division of treasure were spelled out in the license.

De Soto was a leader of experience and resolve. The expedition's chronicler characterized him as "an inflexible man, and dry of word, who, although he liked to know what the others all thought and had to say, after he once said a thing he did not like to be opposed, and as he ever acted as he thought best, all bent to his will." This likeness was published in Antonio Herrera y Tordesillas's Historia General, 1728. No authentic portrait is known to exist.

The King was to have one-fifth of all spoils of battle, one-fifth of any revenue derived from mining precious metals, and one-tenth of all loot taken from graves, sepulchres, Indian temples. Once the region had been explored, De Soto was to become the governor of whatever 200 leagues of coastal area he picked out. There he was to found colonies and build three fortified harbors. He was to pacify the Indians and provide the necessary number of priests and friars to convert them. He was to bear the entire costs of the expedition. When it was over, he would receive, in addition to his share of any booty and a grant of land 12 leagues square (about 50,000 acres), a salary of 2,000 ducats a year, roughly $60,000 today.

The expedition, its quota of men more than filled with volunteers who supplied their own armor and arms, landed in Cuba in June 1538 and spent nearly a year there while De Soto attended to administrative duties and organized the *entrada*. He used far more care than Narváez had. While scouts searched for a good harbor on Florida's west coast, the commissary department rustled up many loads of hard ship biscuit, 5,000 bushels of maize, quantities of bacon, and a herd of rangy hogs. They also brought with them long, clanking strands of iron chains and collars, portents of things to come.

The chronicles of the expedition give different figures about the numbers involved, but this is a reasonable approximation: close to 700 men, perhaps a hundred camp followers, including a few women, many slaves, eight ecclesiastical persons, and 240 or so horses. Having learned from Cabeza de Vaca about some of Narváez's mistakes, De Soto included among the soldiers several artisans capable of working with their hands. People, horses, hogs, and big dogs that could be used for attacking Indians, and a confusion of supplies and equipment were loaded aboard five low-waisted, high-pooped, square-rigged ships ranging from 500 to 800 tons burden. Overflow was accommodated, uncomfortably, in two caravels and two small pinnaces.

The fleet spent a week in late May 1539, reaching the southernmost part of what is generally believed to have been Tampa Bay.* While the ships were groping over the shoals so that unloading could begin, patrols of both horsemen and footmen, happy to be free of the cramped quarters, dashed off through the

*Such is the conclusion of the U.S. De Soto Commission headed by John R. Swanton (*Final Report*, Washington, D.C., 1939), which was appointed by President Roosevelt to study the explorer's route to commemorate the 400th anniversary of the landing, an opinion affirmed by two other scholars, Charles Hudson and Jerald T. Milanich. For a contrary opinion that favors the Fort Myers area, see R.F. Schell, *De Soto Didn't Land at Tampa*, Fort Myers Beach, 1966). Jeffery P. Brain in a new edition of the report for the Smithsonian Press (1985) concludes that the most we can now say is that De Soto landed somewhere along the central Florida gulf coast, "between the Caloosahatchie River to south and the vicinity of Tampa Bay to the north." It is conceivable that future archeological studies will narrow down the landing site.

undergrowth to learn what lay ahead. They soon discovered that the countryside, though sweet-smelling with flowers, was a maze of bogs, meandering streams, and thick stands of mangroves and oaks. Another tax on travel were small groups of tall, naked Indians, probably Timucuans. The Indians eluded the horsemen by dodging nimbly through swamps and behind trees, now and then letting an arrow flash out from one of their bows. Fortunately one of the few captives the patrols seized was Juan Ortiz, a former member of the ill-fated Narváez expedition.

Ortiz had returned to Cuba with the explorer's ships after they had failed to make contact with the land party and then had been hired by Narváez's distraught wife to search for her husband in a pinnace she provided. On visiting Narváez's initial landing place at Tampa Bay, Ortiz had been captured and had lived ever since with a group that controlled part of the region around the bay. He knew the Timucuans' language and could speak through interpreters to other Indian groups. But in all that time he had never been far afield and could report only rumors about distant places. Gold? There was none near at hand, but far to the north was a powerful kingdom abounding in maize. Its inhabitants might know of minerals.

A scouting party dispatched to investigate returned with a tantalizing message that would be repeated over and over during the long trek: the gold was somewhere else, this time at a place called Cale, where the warriors wore golden helmets. De Soto nodded complacently. In a region as vast as Florida, he told the Gentleman of Elvas, there were bound to be riches.

Mindful still of the colony he was supposed to found, he left Pedro Calderón near Tampa Bay with three small ships, their sailors, and a hundred soldiers. They had two years' supply of food and seed for planting. If he found a better place to settle, he would let them know. Meanwhile the other caravel and the five big ships were to return to Havana for fresh supplies and new recruits.

Moving inland farther than Narváez had and marching in divisions, the army moved north. Tough going. Rains were heavy that year. Bogs oozed; lakes and streams rose. The wayfarers waded some streams and bridged others. The men herded the pigs through the mud—the sows had farrowed and there were about 300 now—grooming horses, setting up wet camps and then, tired out, pulverizing, in curved log mortars, the grain they had taken from Indian fields and storage cribs so they could boil it into gruel. Discontent boiled up. There'd better be gold somewhere in this hellhole.

There was none at Cale, but a little farther on. . . They straggled through the vicinity of today's Gainesville and, inclining a little west of north, reached a village called Aguacaliquen. There an advance party captured several women, one of whom was the daughter of the cacique, or chief. The father was told he could not get her back until he had guided the Spaniards into the territory of the next tribe to the west. This he did while several of his villagers followed, playing on bone flutes as a sign of peace and begging that father and daughter be released.

When pleas produced nothing—De Soto feared being left in the wilderness with no guides—the Indians decided to ambush the Spaniards at "a very pleasant village" called Napituca, near today's Live Oak, Florida. De Soto's interpreter, Juan Ortiz, discovered the plot and gave warning. Spirits leaped. After two months of being harassed by Indian guerrillas, the Spaniards could at last vent their frustration on a massed army—about 400 Indians, as it turned out. Giving thanks to God, the cavalry charged, lances thrusting, swords slashing. Bellow of arquebuses, zings of crossbow darts, yells of "Santiago!" from pike-wielding foot soldiers. Scores of Indians died; hundreds were captured, including a remnant that fled into two nearby lakes and, by hiding in the cold, night-shrouded waters, evaded capture until morning—a brave stand that won both admiration and kind treatment from the Spanish force.

Not all the captives were handled that generously. Their services were needed. During marches males were linked by chains and iron collars and forced to serve as porters for the army. Women, historian Garcilaso de la Vega wrote after talking to participants in the adventure, served as "domestics," grinding the rations of maize, cooking the meals, and so on. Rodrigo Ranjel, De Soto's private secretary, was more specific: the soldiers desired women for "foul use and lewdness." Whenever the conquerors seized a new village, its cacique was impressed as a hostage and guide and released only after his subjects had served as bearers over the next stretch of the journey. Rebels against the enslavement received punishments designed to warn other recalcitrants. Some had a hand or nose cut off, a few were tied to stakes and burned or shot to death with arrows fired by Indian auxiliaries. Now and then one was torn to pieces by the Spaniard's war dogs. They accepted the ordeals with a stoicism that won the grudging approval of the expedition's chroniclers.

In October 1539, De Soto's army entered the land of the Apalachees. According to Ranjel, they found "much maize and beans and squash and diverse fruits and many deer and a great diversity of birds and fish." Like Narváez before them, they decided to winter at the fruitful spot, site of today's Tallahassee.

They evicted the Indians of the main town, Anhaica, and settled down in the log and straw houses. Taking advantage of a high wind, the Indians burned most of the place. Later, the intense cold killed almost all of the despondent Indian slaves captured at the battle of Napituca. In spite of the misfortunes, De Soto decided to use Apalachee as a center for future explorations. He sent Juan de Añasco and 30 cavalrymen south through bogs and sniping Indians to Tampa Bay to bring up Calderón's hundred soldiers and the three small ships. When the vessels arrived at the very harbor from which Narváez had sailed (as revealed by the remnants of the forge and the grisly piles of horse bones) De Soto dispatched the ships west under Francisco Maldonado to find a protected bay to which the reinforcements waiting in Havana could be brought the following summer.

Meanwhile another distraction arose. Working through a chain of interpreters, Juan Ortiz learned from an Indian captive that a truly rich country, Cofitachequi, lay to the northeast, in the vicinity of what is now Camden, South Carolina. Promptly, De Soto decided to take his regrouped army there.

They left on March 3, 1540. Because most of their captives had died, the men again had to carry their own rations and prepare their own meals. Spring-swollen streams blocked the way; one was so wide the men built a ferry and hauled it back and forth with hawsers. The cacique of Cofitachequi turned out to be a woman. Bedecked in furs, feathers, and the freshwater pearls that were common in the mussels of the southeast, she greeted them warmly. "Be

The only site linked with certainty to De Soto is *Anhaica*, once the principal town of the Apalachee Indians.

This numerous and powerful people resisted the Spaniards' intrusion into their country in autumn 1539, harassing the march and burning villages to deny food to the army. At *Anhaica* De Soto found an abandoned town of "250 large and good houses." The Spaniards settled in and spent five months here. They scoured the country-side for provisions, seizing quantities of maize, pumpkins, beans, and dried persimmons. The Indians raided the town twice and set fires. When the army departed in spring, they carried enough maize to last them across 200 miles of wilderness.

The exact site of *Anhaica* lay unknown for 450 years. It was discovered by accident in 1987 by archeologist Calvin Jones while searching in downtown Tallahassee, Florida, for a 17th-century Spanish mission. Digging on land planned for development, he and others recovered many 16th-century Spanish artifacts (iron, coins, olive jar fragments, beads, the mandible of a pig) in context with Apalachee pottery. Analysis left no doubt that this was the site of De Soto's first winter camp.

*Artifacts from the Tallahassee site: bits of chain mail (top left), an arrow point (above); a copper coin minted in Spain between 1505-17; the metal tip of a cross bow dart. Digging also turned up fragments of olive jars of the type shown at left. The chain mail shirt at center above shows the type of body armor worn by Spaniards in the first decades of the New World conquest. The jar and shirt were not found at the site.*

43

this coming to these shores most happy," she said according to one chronicler. "My ability can in no way equal my wishes, nor my services [equal] the merits of so great a prince; nevertheless, good wishes are to be valued more than the treasures of the earth without them. With sincerest and purest good will, I tender you my person, my lands, my people, and make you these small gifts."

She gave De Soto strands of freshwater pearls and let the men take more from tombs located in mounds raised above the ground. They were not very good pearls and had been discolored by being bored with redhot copper spindles. But they were the closest things to treasure the men had found so far, and De Soto filled a cane chest with 350 pounds of them.

Won by the pearls, the lush countryside, and the navigability of the Wateree-Santee Rivers, which drained southeast into the Atlantic, the men wanted to found a colony there. De Soto refused. There was not enough food at Cofitachequi for the army. Moreover, he was still hoping, in the words of the Gentleman of Elvas, for another windfall "like that of Atabalipa [Atahualpa] of Peru."

The place to investigate, he heard, was off across the Appalachian Mountains to the northwest. Seizing the cacique who had befriended him, he forced her to enlist a portion of her subjects as porters and domestics for the disgruntled men. They moved rapidly through South Carolina into western North Carolina. By trails that had never before seen a horse, let alone a herd of pigs, they crossed the mountains into the tumbled region of the French Broad and Pigeon Rivers. There the cacique of the pearls managed to escape. As usual, there was no gold.

Hoping, presumably, to meet the ships coming from Havana with supplies and reinforcements, De Soto at last turned south through the land that Creek Indians later occupied in northern Alabama. As they traveled down the Coosa River, they entered a new chiefdom and there laid hold of a tall, disdainful leader named Tascaluza. De Soto demanded women and slaves. With pretended meekness Tascaluza provided the army with a hundred porters and then secretly sent word ahead to his warriors in the stockaded town of Mabila, from which today's Mobile takes its name, to prepare an ambush. When the town came into sight, De Soto carelessly let the main part of the

The female cacique of Cofitachequi, apparently a woman of considerable authority, greeted De Soto's army with ceremony and gifts of food and clothing. Though she had befriended the expedition, she was seized as a hostage and guide but eventually escaped. Artist Louis S. Glanzman illustrates the cacique as she may have appeared at the time of the encounter.

hungry army disperse to forage. Leaving the fettered bearers outside the entrance, the general and a handful of aides entered the village with Tascaluza. Hot words soon broke out, and the Indians hurled themselves at the enemy. The Spaniards clustered around their leader. Although five were killed and De Soto was knocked down a time or two, they managed to fight their way back outside. During the uproar the porters picked up the food, armaments, and other baggage they had been carrying and rushed inside the stockade with it, to join Tascaluza's people.

Assembling his soldiers, De Soto launched attacks against all sides of the barricaded town. With axes and fire the yelling Spaniards smashed through the palisades. While the battle raged from house to house, the tinder-box town went up in flames. Realizing they were being defeated, some of the Indians threw themselves into the fire rather than surrender. The last survivor hanged himself with his bowstring. Reports of Spanish losses range from 18 to 22 killed and 148 wounded, including De Soto. Somewhere between 7 and 12 irreplaceable horses perished and 28 were injured. Indian losses were estimated by a chronicler at 2,500.

Since landing at Tampa Bay, the Spaniards had lost 102 men from all causes. The chest of pearls De Soto had hoped to send to Cuba as a lure for replacements had disappeared in the fire, along with most of the army's spare clothing, weapons, and food. Yet when the interpreter, Juan Ortiz, told De Soto of Indian reports of ships in Mobile Bay a few days away, he ordered him to stay silent. He knew the men would desert if they thought they could reach the ships, and his pride could not tolerate that. Go home empty-handed, beaten, and disgraced? Never.

He rallied the army. For 28 days the healthy doctored the wounded with, said Garcilaso de la Vega, unguents made from the fat of dead Indians. Their commander moved among them, bolstering their spirits, so that when he ordered them to face north again, they obeyed, though they all knew that ships from Havana had been scheduled to meet them somewhere.

They followed the Tombigbee River into northeastern Mississippi to Chicaza, where they wintered (1540-41) among the Chickasaw Indians. When they made their usual request for porters, women, clothing, and food for the spring march, the Chickasaws responded

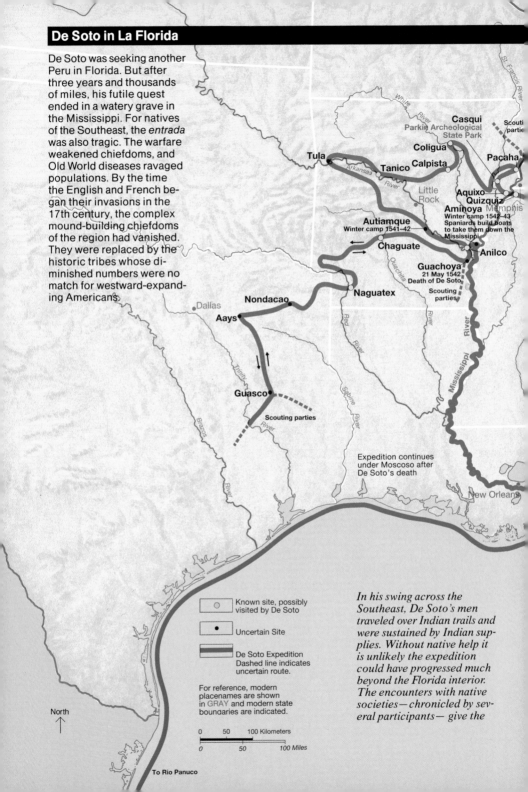

# De Soto in La Florida

De Soto was seeking another Peru in Florida. But after three years and thousands of miles, his futile quest ended in a watery grave in the Mississippi. For natives of the Southeast, the *entrada* was also tragic. The warfare weakened chiefdoms, and Old World diseases ravaged populations. By the time the English and French began their invasions in the 17th century, the complex mound-building chiefdoms of the region had vanished. They were replaced by the historic tribes whose diminished numbers were no match for westward-expanding Americans.

St. Francis River

Scouting parties

White River

Casqui
Parkin Archeological State Park

Tula

Coligua

Arkansas River

Tanico

Calpista

Pacaha

Little Rock

Aquixo
Quizquiz
Aminoya
Winter camp 1542–43
Spaniards build boats to take them down the Mississippi

Memphis

Autiamque
Winter camp 1541–42

Chaguate

Ouachita River

Anilco

Guachoya
21 May 1542
Death of De Soto
Scouting parties

Naguatex

Dallas

Nondacao

Aays

Red River

Ouachita River

Mississippi River

Guasco

Scouting parties

Trinity River

Sabine River

Brazos River

Expedition continues under Moscoso after De Soto's death

New Orleans

North
↑

⊙ Known site, possibly visited by De Soto

● Uncertain Site

De Soto Expedition
Dashed line indicates uncertain route.

For reference, modern placenames are shown in GRAY and modern state boundaries are indicated.

0    50    100 Kilometers
0    50    100 Miles

To Rio Panuco

*In his swing across the Southeast, De Soto's men traveled over Indian trails and were sustained by Indian supplies. Without native help it is unlikely the expedition could have progressed much beyond the Florida interior. The encounters with native societies—chronicled by several participants— give the*

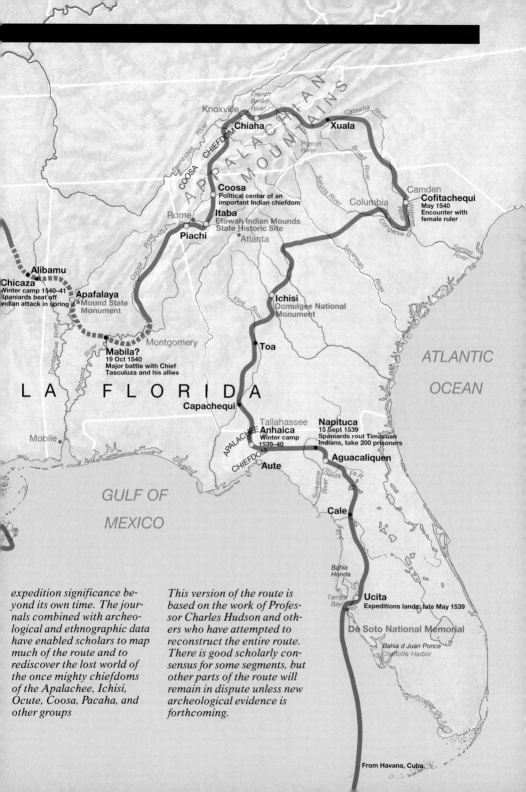

Knoxville

French
Broad
River

Chiaha

Xuala

Catawba River

APPALACHIAN MOUNTAINS

Tennessee River

Pigeon River

COOSA CHIEFDOM

**Coosa**
Political center of an
important Indian chiefdom

Broad River

Saluda River

Camden
**Cofitachequi**
May 1540
Encounter with
female ruler

Columbia

Rome

**Itaba**
Etowah Indian Mounds
State Historic Site

Congaree R.

Wateree River

Santee River

**Piachi**

Atlanta

Coosa River

Savannah River

**Alibamu**

**Chicaza**
Winter camp 1540–41
Spaniards beat off
Indian attack in spring

**Apafalaya**
Mound State
Monument

**Ichisi**
Ocmulgee National
Monument

Flint River

Tombigbee River

Alabama River

**Mabila?**
19 Oct 1540
Major battle with Chief
Tasculuza and his allies

Montgomery

**Toa**

**ATLANTIC
OCEAN**

L A   F L O R I D A

**Capachequi**

Mobile

Tallahassee

**Anhaica**
Winter camp
1539–40

**Napituca**
15 Sept 1539
Spaniards rout Timacuan
Indians, take 200 prisoners

APALACHEE CHIEFDOM

**Aute**

**Aguacaliquen**

Santa Fe R.

Suwannee River

Santa Fe R.

**GULF OF
MEXICO**

**Cale**

Bahia
Honda

Tampa
Bay

**Ucita**
Expeditions lands, late May 1539

De Soto National Memorial

Bahia d Juan Ponce
Charlotte Harbor

expedition significance beyond its own time. The journals combined with archeological and ethnographic data
have enabled scholars to map
much of the route and to
rediscover the lost world of
the once mighty chiefdoms
of the Apalachee, Ichisi,
Ocute, Coosa, Pacaha, and
other groups

This version of the route is
based on the work of Profes-
sor Charles Hudson and others who have attempted to
reconstruct the entire route.
There is good scholarly con-
sensus for some segments, but
other parts of the route will
remain in dispute unless new
archeological evidence is
forthcoming.

From Havana, Cuba

one day at dawn by setting fire to the section of the town in which the invaders were bivouacked. The confusion was total—and perhaps a salvation for the Spaniards. Several terrified horses broke loose and stampeded wildly. Their squeals and the pounding of their hooves, and the sight of De Soto and a few others who had managed to get mounted bearing down on them with lances (before De Soto's saddle turned and he fell heavily) frightened the Indians into flight.

It was a disaster, nevertheless. Twelve soldiers and a white woman still with the army—she was pregnant—were dead as were several score pigs and 57 horses, the latter mourned as deeply as the men, for they were the army's true strength. But once again, they rallied, improvised forges for retempering their weapons, replaced the shafts of their lances, and learned to patch their clothing with woven grasses, pounded bark, and pieces of Indian blankets.

On May 9 or so, 1541, after more battles, they reached the Mississippi at—no one knows, but it seems to have been south of Memphis. While they were marveling at the river's size (this is from Elvas), 200 dugout canoes approached in perfect order. In each canoe warriors, painted with ochre and bedecked with plumes of many colors, stood erect, protecting the oarsmen with feathered shields and bows and arrows. The chief man of the fleet sat in his canoe underneath an awning and likewise each lesser chief in his canoe. The Spaniards had seen panoply before—bearers carrying their caciques on feathered litters while flute players marched beside—but nothing like this. Misunderstood stories of such spectacles, as we will see later, caused considerable trouble for the expedition Mendoza sent north under Coronado during this same period.

A brief parley between the cacique and De Soto ended when nervous crossbowmen, misreading what was going on, shot five or six of the Indians. At once the fleet withdrew, still in perfect order, "like a famous armada of galleys," wrote Elvas. What follows passes understanding. In spite of clear warnings not to proceed, De Soto decided to go ahead. During the next hot, humid month, the men felled trees, sawed them into planks, and constructed barges. To avoid detection, they crossed the river, with the horses aboard, in the pre-dawn darkness of June 18 and moved northwest.

*The Indians valued the brass bells and brightly colored glass beads given them by the Spaniards. Where found, they help authenticate Spanish presence in the 16th century. These examples were excavated in Florida.*

They spent most of the summer and fall wandering around western Arkansas. Many scholars believe they may have traveled up the Arkansas River almost to eastern Oklahoma before going into their 1541-42 winter quarters in a town (Autiamque) once again commandeered from the Indians. Though the weather was severe, the men stayed fairly snug. Their slaves built a strong stockade around the camp and dragged in ample supplies of firewood. Local Indians provided them with buffalo robes to use as overcoats and to sleep on, and showed them how to snare the rabbits that frequented the nearby cornfields.

During the long days inside the stockade, De Soto at last faced up to his situation. He had lost half his force. Not all had died in battle. A few, despairing of seeing the end of the quest, had deserted to live with the Indians, and the number would increase if he persisted in wandering as he had been doing. Of the original 223 horses, only 40 remained, most of them lame for want of shoes. The death of Juan Ortiz that winter deprived him of his best, if very uncertain, means of communication with the Indians. Reluctantly he decided to turn back to Mississippi. There he intended to build two brigantines and, manning them with his most trustworthy men, send one to Havana and one to Pánuco in hope that one would be able to lead reinforcements back to those who would wait for them at the river.

They reached the roily Mississippi somewhere near the mouth of the Arkansas River. By that time a deadly fever, perhaps malaria, was gnawing at De Soto. Knowing death was near and bitterly resenting the arrogant hostility of the Indians with whom he tried to treat in his extremity, he ordered two of his captains to go out with lancers and infantry and make an example of the nearby town of Anilco. Not expecting an attack, for they had not been among those taking the lead in defying the Spaniards, the unarmed townspeople clustered about in curiosity. A wanton butchery followed. "About one hundred men were slain," wrote Elvas. "Many were allowed to get away badly wounded, that they might strike terror into those who were absent." Eighty women and children were taken prisoner.

By the time the bloodletting was over, De Soto could not rise from his bed. After confessing his sins and making his will, he named Luís de Moscoso as

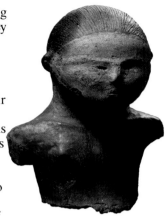

*This effigy from a gourd-shaped ceramic vessel was discovered in a burial at Ocmulgee National Monument in central Georgia. De Soto's expedition passed near this site.*

his successor. On May 21, 1542, he died.

To keep the Indians from knowing the fate of the great Child of the Sun, as he had been describing himself to them, his followers buried him near the entrance to the town and rode horses back and forth to destroy signs of the digging. The Indians were suspicious, however, and so Moscoso had the corpse disinterred, lest the Indians dig it up and mutilate it. A handful of men then stealthily wrapped the body in a shroud, weighted the burden with sand, and in the darkness of the night rowed out onto the river and dumped it overboard.

De Soto's plan to build boats for bringing in reinforcements died with him. The men's one desire now was to leave this country that had brought them only misery. But how? Remembering Narváez's fate, they were reluctant to try to build enough boats to carry them home by sea. Instead they decided to march overland to Pánuco in northern Mexico. They clung to the decision for four months, fighting off Indians when they had to and living off the country as they had been doing ever since the landing at Tampa Bay. Then, as the subtropical growth began to give way to the desert scrub of south central Texas, they encountered, in a village of poor huts, a woman who said, or they thought she said, that she had seen Christians at a place nine days' travel away and that "she had been in their hands, but had escaped." Moscoso sent a squad of cavalrymen with her in the direction she indicated, but when she contradicted herself, or they thought she did, they abandoned the quest.

The Spaniards were losing heart. They could not live off this land of semi-nomadic Indians where little maize grew. As winter approached, the idea of travel by sea no longer seemed so forbidding. Wheeling around, they regained the Mississippi in two months of hard travel over the same trails they had come and in December seized, for use as their fourth winter quarters (1542-43), an Indian town (Aminoya) a little upstream of the one which they had destroyed seven months before.

Good timber surrounded the village, and the few artisans still alive had clung to their tools. They made more nails out of their meager supply of horseshoes and other iron, contrived ropes out of bark, and sails out of shawls collected from the Indians. To escape a flood that sent the river out of its banks, they put

*Mississippian culture in the Southeast (AD 1000-1600) evolved a rich artistic tradition. The items on these pages come from the area De Soto marched through. The effigy vessel (7.5 inches high) and the stone axe (13 inches long) opposite are representative of this culture in Arkansas. The axe, which is carved from a single piece of stone, was probably a badge of office. The artist's stone palette (12.5 inches in diameter) was found at Etowah Mounds State Historic Site, Georgia. The engraving has been interpreted as snake emissaries of the sun god, which is represented by the eye.*

their horses on anchored rafts and saved themselves by climbing to the tops of their huts. Indians kept paddling around their refuge in canoes. Suspicious of their intent, Moscoso had one of his men seize a native. Under torture the fellow said that 20 chiefs of the surrounding tribes were conspiring to attack the invaders. A sign would be the approach of Indians bearing gifts of fish to lull the camp into relaxing its guard. When the native chiefs showed up with fish as predicted, the Spanish laid hold of them, cut off each man's right hand, and sent the victims back to their villages to report that their scheme was known. Although some of the chiefs persisted in their intrigues, Moscoso, very much on guard now, was able to outwit them, force submission, and acquire through it all more heaps of shawls out of which to make sails.

By July the fleet was ready—seven brigantines and several Indian-style war canoes lashed side by side. They loaded the vessels with casks of fresh water and several hundred bushels of corn scoured from a countryside that could ill afford the loss. During the last days of work they killed and ate the poorest of the horses. The soundest, 22 all told, were put aboard, as were a hundred slaves. The rest of the Indians they had dragged along with them were turned loose in this country where the tribes were hostile to them.

The river journey was a series of violent, if intermittent, battles. Indians from towns they passed swarmed after them in canoes, raining arrows on them. Ten Spaniards and an unknown number of slaves died, and because the horses were slowing their flight, Moscoso at last put ashore at a defensible spot, killed them, and dried the meat.

After 17 days they reached the Gulf, turned west, and on September 10, 1543, after weeks of combatting fretful seas, contrary winds, thirst and hunger, 311 survivors (again not counting captive Indians) reached the Pánuco River. Said Elvas: "Many, leaping ashore, kissed the ground; and all, on bended knees, with hands raised above them and their eyes to Heaven, remained untiring in giving thanks to God."

One of the most extraordinary marches in the annals of the New—or Old—World had come to a profitless end.

# Piachi, Village in the Coosa Chiefdom

After crossing the Great Smokies, De Soto in August 1540 entered the territory of a rich chiefdom called Coosa. It dominated an area from the French Broad River in North Carolina into central Alabama. De Soto's chronicler described this country as "Thickly settled in numerous and large towns, with fields between, extending from one to another, [it] was pleasant and had a rich soil and fair river margins."

One of the subject towns was *Piachi* (the King Site to archeologists), on the banks of the Coosa River in northwest Georgia. De Soto and his expedition spent a day here in early September 1540. The chronicles are silent on the visit, but from the archeological work of David Hally and others, as interpreted by artist L. Kenneth Townsend, we have a good idea of life here.

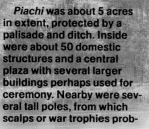

*Piachi* was about 5 acres in extent, protected by a palisade and ditch. Inside were about 50 domestic structures and a central plaza with several larger buildings perhaps used for ceremony. Nearby were several tall poles, from which scalps or war trophies prob-ably hung. About 350 persons lived here, less than half the number of the main town of Coosa or the substantial village of Itaba (Etowah Indian Mounds State Historic Site to the north). A good part of the villagers' living came from growing corn, which they stored in cribs. As the Spaniards traveled from village to village, they expected the Indians to yield up food, guides, porters, and women. Without this sustenance, the expedition could not have covered the territory that it did.

# Where the Fables Ended

*Acoma Pueblo, New Mexico, visited by the Coronado expedition in 1540. It is one of the oldest continuously inhabited communities in the United States.*

Like De Soto, Francisco Vásquez de Coronado* was a younger son who improved his minimal prospects for worldly success by attaching himself to a patron—in this case it was the king's fabulously wealthy viceroy, Antonio de Mendoza—and going with him to the New World. They arrived in 1535, when Coronado was 25.

Because of Mendoza's position and character, Coronado's rise was faster and more genteel than De Soto's. Two years after settling in Mexico City (originally Tenochtitlán), he married Beatriz de Estrada, an heiress whose father had been the illegitimate son of Spain's first king, Ferdinand. About the same time Mendoza arranged for his appointment to Mexico City's governing council and shortly thereafter named him governor of the far northern province of Nueva Galicia. (The position was open because Nuño de Guzmán had been arrested for slave-hunting, and his successor had been killed while fighting Indians.) The only battling Coronado did during those years was putting down a revolt of black slaves in the mining district of Amatepeque. Though he had the rebel leaders drawn and quartered, a standard punishment of the times, he seems to have been more humane than many of his contemporaries.

Even before Coronado's appointment was officially announced, De Soto's agents in Mexico notified him that their employer had become *adelantado* of Florida. In other words, hands off . . . a bluff, since the limits of De Soto's jurisdiction had not been established. But the very fact of the warning shows that De Soto and his people were suspicious of how the winds might be blowing in Mexico.

They had reason to be. Mendoza had finally put together a reconnoitering party whose early entrance into the desirable area would give him a prior claim over either De Soto or Cortés. Take-off point for the group was to be Culiacán, an outpost on the western fringe of Nueva Galicia, 800 miles from Mexico City,

*Because Vásquez was the family name of the *conquistador*, the young man should properly be called Vásquez. This account, however, will follow established American custom and call him Coronado.

that Guzmán had founded a few years earlier. The explorers were hurried across those rough miles by Nueva Galicia's new governor, Francisco de Coronado, and a retinue of restless young blades looking for something to do. From Culiacán on, the scouts were guided by the black, Estéban, who had traversed part of the country with his owner, Andrés de Dorantes, and Cabeza de Vaca. (Mendoza had purchased Estéban from Dorantes after the three whites of the party had turned down the viceroy's request that they take over the work.) Indians of the north—some of them had come to Mexico City with Cabeza de Vaca—acted as porters. Leader of this belatedly assembled group was a Franciscan friar, Marcos of Niza, assisted by a friend, Fray Onorato.

Fray Marcos, a native of Nice, France, spoke Spanish clumsily, even though he had spent time with Pedro de Alvarado's forces in Guatemala and Pizarro's in Peru, where he had become familiar with the astonishing wealth of the Incas. He is said to have been a good cartographer and to have written learned papers about the Indians, none of which has come to light. He penned such an entrancing letter about Peru to Mexico's Archbishop, Juan de Zumárraga, that the prelate invited him to visit Mexico City and housed him after his arrival early in 1537. The impression he made led the archbishop to arrange his appointment to an important office in the Franciscan order in New Spain, and the viceroy to make him leader of the search for the cities of the north.

Coronado and his escort covered the 800 miles to Culiacán on horseback, as befitted grandees. Marcos's party walked, the friars in loose gray robes and sandaled feet. After bidding farewell to the governor at the outpost, the explorers and their Indian porters forged ahead on March 7, 1539. (In two more months De Soto would leave Cuba for Florida.) Fray Onorato soon fell ill and turned back. Undeterred, Marcos continued on to a settlement called Vacapa, close to the boundary between the present-day states of Sinaloa and Sonora. There he decided to pause while messengers summoned Indians from the coast, for part of his errand was to learn whether a big expedition could be supplied by ships.

Estéban refused to wait. Away from the friar's restraints, he ceased being a slave and became a king. During his wanderings across the continent he had learned how to get along with Indians, speak their languages, win their gifts, and (we can suppose) entice their young women. But he dared not simply run away. So he said that as he advanced, accompanied by two huge hounds and part of the Indian bearers, he would keep Marcos informed of his gleanings. Unable to write, he devised a symbol that could be delivered by messengers. A small cross would signify that he had heard of a northern city that sounded moderately important. A medium-sized cross would proclaim a significant city, and a big one something truly superlative.

Presumably this tactic was devised to corroborate what the messengers told Marcos to his face. Told him—this man who knew none of the local Indian tongues and whose Spanish was not of the best? How?

Actually, it would have been easy, except for Marcos's dangerous preconceptions. A long trade trail linked the jungles of Mexico to the merchandising town of Háwikuh in the Zuñi country of today's New Mexico. Háwikuh's middlemen trans-shipped along the trail tanned buffalo hides from the plains, turquoise from New Mexico, cotton mantas from the Hopi villages in Arizona, and bits of clear green olivine called peridot (the source perhaps of Cabeza de Vaca's lost arrowheads). They received in exchange brightly colored parrot and macaw feathers and sometimes the birds themselves, plus coral and raw carved seashells from the Gulf. Flowing with the goods was a traders' *lingua franca*, a melange of the principal languages the merchants encountered along the way—their own native tongue, bits of that spoken by the Pimas and Opatas of northern Mexico, Nahuatl, the tongue of the Aztecs, and bits of Spanish. So there was a medium by which Estéban's messengers, especially the one who brought a cross as big as a man, could talk to the eager friar.

From the cross's bearers and from other informants along the way, Marcos heard of, and sent back reports to Mendoza, about the rich kingdom called Cíbola and its seven cities, one of which, he understood, was also named Cíbola. Terraced houses of stone rose three and four stories high. Doors were decorated with turquoise; clothing and ornaments were lavish. Near to this magnificent kingdom were others, equally rich.

Mere travelers' yarns? Not necessarily. Consider

*Antonio de Mendoza, first viceroy of New Spain. A capable administrator, he laid the foundations for three centuries of Spanish rule in the Americas. He encouraged industry, education, and the work of the church. Firm but just, he tried to protect the Indians from the worst abuses but was not able to bring about emancipation.*

**Next page** *Coronado saw country like this south of Santa Fe, New Mexico, as he marched toward the Great Plains.*

who Estéban's messengers were. They resided in small, trailside settlements made up of *jacals* built of mud-daubed sticks. In comparison, the terraced pueblos of Arizona and New Mexico, inhabited by hundreds of people who had sufficient leisure to attend to other pursuits than just getting enough to eat—such places, which most of them had only heard about from boastful peddlers, were bound to seem impressive. Talking through interpreters in signs and their *lingua franca* jumble, they tried to convey their wonder to Marcos—as did one person who said he was a native of Cíbola and apparently enjoyed bragging about it. While listening, moreover, Marcos was remembering the Incas and Aztecs and the legends of the Seven Cities of Antilia. Seven in Cíbola as well! Whose imagination would not be fired?

He never overtook Estéban. According to his report to Mendoza, he and his retinue of Indians had been toiling for 12 days across a *despoblado* (uninhabited region) and were within three days' march of the city of Cíbola when one of the black's erstwhile companions met them and said, weeping, that the Cíbolans had slain Estéban out of fear that he had come as a spy for would-be conquerors—as, in fact, he had. Two days later, the tale was confirmed by other Indians who had fled from Cíbola "covered with blood and many wounds."

Convinced they were walking to their deaths, all but a handful of Marcos's followers deserted him. With those few, he wrote later, he went cautiously forward until he glimpsed the city. It rose before his eyes more magnificent "than the city of Mexico." And equally wealthy kingdoms lay beyond.

Deciding to rename Cíbola St. Francis after the patron saint of his order, Marcos erected a heap of stones, placed a cross atop it, and announced to the air that he was taking possession for Spain. Then back he hastened, "more satiated with fear than food." So he said.

Skeptics have long argued that Fray Marcos never got anywhere near Cíbola. They point to the vagueness of his report, which nowhere describes topographical features, vegetation, or soil types, although his instructions had directed him to study all those things. They also insist that he could not have tarried in Indian towns and have made side trips searching for the coast, as he claimed he did, and still have reached and returned from Cíbola in the time known to have elapsed. And how could he have mistaken a relatively small, mud-plastered pueblo for a metropolis grander than Mexico City?

Supporters of the friar, unwilling to believe a man of the cloth could be an out-and-out liar, juggle time figures their own way and suggest that his impression of the pueblo was an optical illusion produced by slanting rays of morning sunlight and made more vivid by the mixture of weariness, excitement, hope, and fear with which he regarded his goal. They also point out that when a full-scale expedition marched north to take possession of the country, he went along. Would he have done that if his statements were lies that would inevitably be exposed?

It seems likely that he did turn back immediately after learning, at some distance from Cíbola, of Estéban's death. But vanity and fear of consequences would not let him admit the truth to the viceroy and the governor. So he concocted a tale out of the descriptions he had heard from Indians along the way—descriptions he believed, reasonably enough, were accurate and would bear scrutiny later on.

His temporal superiors accepted his statements partly out of an eager credulity of their own and partly because they were in a hurry to complete their claims to the Seven Cities. (De Soto was already in Florida; three ships outfitted by Cortés and commanded by Francisco de Ulloa were tacking north along the coast looking for sea approaches to the new kingdoms.) It has even been charged that the viceroy, Mendoza, may have suggested some of the glowing details that were incorporated into Marcos's report. Most certainly he rewarded the friar by pressuring the Order of St. Francis to make him, rather than candidates who had been around much longer, the father-provincial of the Franciscans in Mexico. As a result, pulpits began resounding with homilies on the work that awaited the pious—and, by implication, the enterprising—in the north. This of course stimulated recruiting, not only of idle *hidalgos* but of solid men with money enough to equip themselves and their followers for an extensive journey.

Mendoza reputedly put 60,000 ducats into the venture. Coronado added 50,000 that he raised by mortgaging his wife's property. But they were not completely reckless. They ordered Melchior Díaz,

mayor of Culiacán, to go north with soldiers and
Indians and gather specifics about geography that
Marcos had neglected to describe (not having seen
it) but that an army on the march would find useful.

By February 22, 1540, less than seven months after
Marcos's return, Mendoza and Coronado had gathered the bulk of their army at Nueva Galicia's drab
capital, Compostela, some 525 miles west of Mexico
City. For the place and times it was a brave show:
about 225 cavalrymen, 62 foot soldiers, an unrecorded
number of black slaves, and upwards of 700 variously
painted Indians. The group's equipment, like that of
De Soto's army, was a melange. There were a few
suits of armor, including Coronado's gilded one, some
cuirasses, coats of mail, and plumed helmets but far
more jackets of buckskin and padded cotton, high
boots, and leather shields.

The Indians were camptenders, stockherders, and
warriors, but not bearers, for unlike De Soto,
Mendoza and Coronado meant to enforce royal orders that forbade turning natives into beasts of burden. Some of the Indians had wives and children
along, as did three Spaniards, in spite of edicts against
camp followers. Hardly noticeable in the throng were
five gray-robed friars, including Marcos, who probably should not have left his new job as Father Supe-
rior so soon. Yet he, too, had a big stake in this trip.

Some 1,500 saddle and pack animals, both horses
and mules, had been gathered to provide transporta-
tion. Many of the cavalrymen had more than one
mount; Coronado took along 23. Each soldier was
responsible for his personal gear, and since few
*hidalgos* had the least idea of how to pack a horse,
many impromptu rodeos occurred. But "in the end,"
wrote chronicler Pedro de Castañeda, "necessity,
which is all-powerful, made them skillful . . . and any-
body who despised this work was not considered a
man." In addition to the horse herd, there was a
movable larder of about a thousand cattle, sheep,
and goats.

Though Mendoza had planned to lead the expedition, the demands of his office prevented it, and he
turned command over to Coronado, then aged 30.
The next day the confused, dusty march began, over
high hills and through vales full of thickets. Trouble
awaited at Chiametla, where once Cortés and Guzmán
had confronted each other over a ship. Resentful

Indians attacked a foraging party led by Coronado's second-in-command, killed him, and wounded five or six others. On top of that, in came Melchoir Díaz with discouraging reports of what he had learned during his scouting trip. Though heavy snow had kept him from entering the mountains north of Arizona's Gila River, he had interviewed several Indian traders who supposedly knew Cíbola, and they had led him to believe there was little, if any, silver or gold in the area. And the road there, which Marcos had said was good, was very bad.

Rumors of the report leaked out and upset the soldiers. Marcos quieted them during one of his sermons: Díaz hadn't gone far enough. A preacher's word against that of a frontier roughneck. Coronado, at least, was placated: why let go of either his credulity or his investment this early in the game? But he was worried about dragging the whole cumbersome army over a bad trail into a *despoblado* lacking in supplies. So he decided to go ahead with a vanguard of 80 horsemen, 30 or so footmen, an unknown number of Indians, some livestock, and the expedition's five friars. He placed the main army under Tristan de Arellano, told him to stay in Culiacán for 20 more days and then advance to the Indian town of Corazones in the heart of Sonora, where further instructions would be sent him.

It took Coronado's vanguard from April 22 to July 7, 1540—eleven weeks, counting rest stops—to cover the thousand miles that separated Culiacán from Cíbola. (During those same weeks De Soto's hungry men were marching through Georgia into the city of pearls and on across the Appalachians into Alabama.) Hard weeks on rough trails. Contrary to what Marcos had said, they were veering farther and farther from the coast. Yet at that very time, Hernando de Alarcón was sailing northward with three ships loaded with supplies for him. How were they to make contact?

As events developed, they never did, and the vanguard crossed the shimmering San Pedro plains into what was to be the United States with an increasing apprehension that all gates were shutting behind them. They followed the tree-shaded San Pedro River north to the vicinity of Benson, Arizona, and then, with Melchior Díaz pointing the way, left it and worked on through a series of broad-bottomed, mountain-bracketed valleys to the Gila River, reach-

# First Blood at Cíbola

At Cíbola, Coronado had his first encounter with the Pueblo world. His army was six months into the expedition and worn down from crossing a wilderness. Food was short, his porters (blacks) and Indians were deserting, horses were dying of exhaustion.

The first sight of Cíbola—the legendary kingdom of the north—dismayed the Spaniards. They found not a shining city of gold but only mud huts stacked one atop another and a crowd of armed warriors. This was Háwikuh, western-most of a cluster of Zuñi towns, now a ruin a few miles south of the present pueblo of the same name.

Wanting food, Coronado sent forward a party with an interpreter, friars, and cavalry. This is the moment illustrated by artist Louis S. Glanzman. The interpreter tells Háwikuh's war leaders that the Spaniards have come to claim the country for King and Savior and wish them no harm. The Indians pay this no attention. An elder draws a line of sacred corn meal in the sand. The Spaniards hesitate. Arrows fly. The army storms the village. Soon a dozen Indians lie dead while the rest flee. The famished soldiers break into the stores. Peace follows and this pueblo becomes Coronado's base camp for the next few months.

ing it where Mt. Turnbull bulks huge against the sky. An enormity of space and remoteness. One can still feel it, for unlike the southeastern United States, where De Soto marched, this land has been but little scarred by man's devouring technologies.

They climbed the rough Gila Mountains, found relief in high, open meadows, but then had to scramble over the Natanes Plateau and pitch down a steep Indian trail into the Black River gorge. On beyond that they came to a more difficult crossing of the *barranca*, as they called the canyon, of the White River. The water was so deep they had to build rafts to get across. Then on through more pines and meadows whose beauty they scarcely noticed. They were so hungry that at one camp they ate lush-looking plants—perhaps wild parsnip, perhaps water hemlocks—that twisted them with cramps; one Spaniard and two blacks perished.

Two days later, amidst bare, rolling hills, they passed the Little Colorado and started up Zuñi Creek. Knowing that Cíbola and its food supplies were near, the men wanted to hurry, but Coronado, ever cautious, sent out scouts under tough Garcia López de Cárdenas, and kept the main force moving slowly behind. Near midnight, Indians attacked the reconnoitering group and stampeded some of its horses. Quelling a brief panic, the invaders swept the Indians aside, but the portent was clear. The Cíbolans were going to defend their homes.

As the Spaniards emerged from a scattering of junipers onto a flat plain, they saw, hardly half a mile away, a low spur protruding from a line of hills. On top of the spur was a city of sorts. Blank tan walls rose three and, in places, four stories high. Clusters of people on top. Cornfields and squat houses at the base of the spur. "There are," Casteñada wrote in disgust, "haciendas in New Spain which make a better appearance at a distance." And he added, "Such were the curses that some hurled at Fray Marcos that I pray God may protect him from them."

Points of view. Modern archeologists have discovered data about the Pueblo (Anasazi) Indians that were unknown to the Spaniards. For one thing, population in general was declining in the 16th century, but towns were growing because survivors were congregating in them, perhaps as a defense against raiding nomads. One major population center was the six, not seven, pueblos of the area now known as the Zuñi reservation, then called Cíbola. (No single "city" had that name; that was just another misunderstanding of Marcos.) The town of Háwikuh lay farthest to the southwest and hence dominated the ancient trade trails leading from the entire Pueblo country to Mexico, the Gulf Coast, and those parts of Southern California bordering on the Pacific. Háwikuh, accordingly—and all Cíbola—seemed important to the inhabitants of a considerable area, a notion Marcos had picked up and relayed to his superiors, as we have seen.

The Spaniards, however, had not come looking for dealers in hides, feathers, and imported sea shells. In spite of doubts and warnings that must have troubled them along the way, it was still impossible for them to adjust in one stunning moment to this thunderclap of reality. They went on doing what they probably would have done if the army of the Grand Khan had advanced to meet them. Cavalrymen made sure their saddle girths were tight, footmen readied their weapons, which had not been well cared for during the march, and together they moved toward the Indians, whose leaders drew magic lines of cornmeal on the ground and blew angrily on conch shell trumpets. With bows and war clubs they gestured for the invaders to leave. No women or children were in sight, and the numbers of warriors indicated that the neighboring towns had sent reinforcements. None seemed awed by the sight of horses.

Dutifully the Spaniards went through the ritual of the *requerimiento*. Cárdenas, a few cavalrymen, a notary, an interpreter, and two priests approached the Indians. The interpreter read a proclamation stating that God's representative, the Pope, had awarded this part of the world to the monarchs of Spain. All who submitted to his majesty's authority and also accepted Christianity with its promises of salvation would be embraced as friends. Those who did not would be treated as enemies.

The answer was a shower of arrows that did no harm. Coronado next went forward, holding out gifts as a sign of peace. Mistaking the offering for timidity, the Indians rushed forward. The invaders countered with a charge. Evidently the horses did inspire terror then, for the Indians broke and fled. Some were downed on the plain, but most gained the town and

## To Pecos and Beyond

Marching from Cibola to Pecos, Alvarado's soldiers saw Puebloland in the morningtide of its history, a time of prosperity and relative peace. Village after village welcomed the Spaniards. At Acoma, built on a mesa, "the natives . . . came down to meet us peacefully" and gave the Spaniards supplies for their journey. In Tiguex province, they met Indians "more devoted to agriculture than to war" who gave them food, cloth, and skins. At the huge pueblo of Braba (present Taos), more hospitality. Cicuyé (Pecos), their destination, greeted Alvarado with drums and flutes and plied the soldiers with clothing and turquoise (but the women kept hidden). The record is clear that when the intruders came peacefully, first encounters were not always hostile.

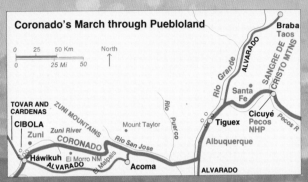

Coronado's March through Puebloland

Roy Anderson

climbed onto the flat roofs, where they continued their gestures of defiance.

Perhaps there was no gold in the town, but there was food and the Spaniards were half-starved. Coronado deployed horsemen entirely around the town to prevent anyone's escaping while he himself dismounted and led an attack on foot up the slope toward the pueblo's single narrow, twisting entry. Clad in gilded armor that attracted attention (and must have been clumsy to run in), he was straightway knocked senseless by a huge stone. Two officers shielded his body while he was dragged to safety.

Advantage of position was with the defenders, and the Spaniards, we are told, were in bad shape. The strings of the crossbows, rotted by the sun, snapped when cranked tight. The arquebusers were too weak from hunger and heat to join the onslaught. Yet no one was killed and only a dozen were hurt. Within less than an hour the town surrendered, an outcome difficult to understand unless the defenders hurled their missiles so wildly that none took effect, whereupon they gave up, terrified by the enemy's relentless momentum and flashing swords, a weapon they had never before encountered.

After Coronado had recovered from his concussion and his men had sated their hunger on Háwikuh's corn, beans, and turkeys (which the Indians raised for feathers rather than food), he began assessing his situation. Couriers brought in delegations from the neighboring towns, and he put what he learned from them into a long letter he wrote Mendoza and dated August 3, 1540. It is a prized ethnographical document now because of its generally accurate descriptions of the Pueblos. Mendoza must have found it discouraging. No gold. But Coronado was determined, he wrote, to keep pressing the search. To strengthen his forces he sent orders, via the letter-bearers, for the bulk of the main army to advance to Háwikuh. The remainder were to establish a halfway station beside the long trail. This station was entrusted to Melchior Díaz. As soon as Díaz had put things in shape there, he was to ride to the Gulf in search of Alarcón's supply ships. Fray Marcos, ill, disgraced, and fearing for his safety, went home with the messengers.

Meanwhile exploring parties had gone northwest from Háwikuh to lay claim to the "kingdom of Tusayan," or, as we would say, the Hopi villages. Noth-

On Cíbola: "Although [the Seven Cities] are not decorated with turquoises, nor made of lime or good bricks, nevertheless they are very good houses, three, four, and five storeys high, and they have very . . . good rooms with corridors, and some quite good apartments underground and paved, which are built for winter and are something like hot-houses [kivas] . . . In [Háwikuh] are perhaps 200 houses, all surrounded by a wall . . . The people of these towns are fairly large and seem to me to be quite intelligent . . . most of them are entirely naked except for the covering required for decency . . . they wear the hair on their heads like the Mexicans, and are well formed and comely . . . the food they eat in this country consists of maize, of which they have a great abundance, beans, and game . . . They make the best tortillas I have ever seen anywhere, and this is what everybody ordinarily eats."
— *Coronado to Mendoza, 3 August 1540*

ing the Spaniards wanted was there, either—except for ill-understood talk about a big river farther to the west. It could be crucial. It must flow into the sea and might furnish a route inland for Alarcón. Promptly Coronado ordered Garcia López de Cárdenas to investigate.

The result was the first sighting, by Europeans, of the Grand Canyon at a point generally believed to have been Desert View. Awed by the chasm, the party explored along the rim until thirst turned them back. Clearly such a stream could not serve as a supply route.

A few weeks later and many hundreds of miles farther downstream Melchior Díaz at last unearthed (literally) the first clues about Hernando de Alarcón's whereabouts. After straightening out affairs at the halfway station named San Gerónimo, he led 25 cavalrymen and some Indians west to the Gulf's torrid coast, driving a herd of sheep along for food. A swing north along the desolate beaches brought him to the banks of a river. He continued along it for perhaps 90 miles, until encountering Indians who showed him where another bearded man like himself had hidden some letters. The documents he dug up have since disappeared, but from other sources it is possible to guess what they said.

Alarcón had reached the river mouth about August 25, 1540. He had been preceded there by Cortés's man, Francisco de Ulloa, who a year earlier had been trying to find an inlet that would enable his commander to beat Mendoza to the Seven Cities. Because Ulloa believed that Baja California was an island, he had been surprised to find himself pinched into the head of a gulf. A most disconcerting place—shoals, seemingly bottomless mudbanks, and a terrifying tidal bore, raging tumults of water caused when the inflowing tide rushed in a great wave upriver against the current.

The sight had turned Ulloa back, but Alarcón was more persistent. He worked a tortuous way through the shoals and, with waves dashing over the deck of his flagship, rode the bore into the channel on August 26. Unable to sail upward against the current, he anchored his three vessels behind a protecting point. Lowering two ship's launches, he ticked off 20 men, some to work the oars, the others to walk along the bank, pulling two ropes. Eventually Cócopa Indians appeared, highly excited. None of them understood the *lingua franca* of his interpreter, but by signs and a passing out of trinkets, Alarcón in time prevailed on them to bring food and to help with the cordelling.

On September 6, two months after the battle at Háwikuh, the slow-moving boats reached, it is believed, a point near the junction of the Colorado and Gila rivers, the site of today's Yuma, Arizona. Nearby, Alarcon's interpreter found Indians with whom he could converse. Their news was startling. Far inland, white men were causing trouble among the native inhabitants. Coronado's army, surely, which Alarcón had been directed to supply. But how?

When none of his own men and none of the Indians would agree to carry a message to Háwikuh, Alarcón decided to return to the ships, take on fresh supplies, and go to Cíbola himself. During the attempt he advanced one day's journey farther upstream than he had gone before, but then physical difficulties and the growing hostility of the Indians forced him to halt. After burying the letter Díaz found, he returned to Mendoza with valuable information about the new land—but, again, no gold.

Having found the letter, Díaz continued upstream for another five or six days, perhaps to learn whether this was indeed the lower end of the big river about which the Hopis had spoken. Evidently satisfied that it was, he sent the Indian footmen of his party and the sheep across the stream on rafts made of reeds. Riders swam over on their horses, and the whole party turned back downstream. At some point in those grisly deserts, Díaz's greyhound began tormenting a sheep. Díaz ran at the dog with his lance. The point stuck in the ground. Before he could stop his horse, the butt pierced his groin. His distraught men put him on a litter, recrossed the river (it is very low in the fall of the year), and hurried toward San Gerónimo, to no avail. He died and was buried no one knows where.

Of the Coronado party's far-flung explorations, the one that had the greatest impact on its future was Hernando de Alvarado's trip to the Great Plains. It was touched off by the appearance at Háwikuh, late in August, of a still undefined party of Indians— traders probably, but perhaps a group who felt they should learn more about what was going on in Cíbola.

They hailed from the pueblo of Cicuyé, located near a river we call Pecos in north-central New Mexico. (Cicuyé was the inhabitants' name for their town; Pecos, now applied to both the river and the pueblo ruins, derives from *Pekush*, a word other Pueblo Indians used in speaking of the settlement.) The travelers were led by an elder whom the Spaniards called *Cacique*, as if it were a name. (Actually, it was an Arawak word meaning "chief." The *conquistadores* had picked it up first in the West Indies and later had applied it to Indian leaders throughout Latin America.) Accompanying Cacique was a husky, talkative young man adorned with drooping mustaches, unusual in an Indian. Coronado's people named him *Bigotes*, or, in English, Whiskers. Bigotes apparently spoke some Nahuatl, which meant he could converse after a fashion with a few of the explorers, notably Father Juan de Padilla, who seems to have been going slowly mad. Another attention-catcher among the visitors was an Indian from the Great Plains who had a painted picture of a buffalo on his bare chest.

Coronado considered the newcomers a peace delegation. He gave them glass trinkets, beads, and little bells that entranced them. They responded with head dresses, shields, and a wooly hide that, they signified, had been taken from an animal like the one pictured on the chest of one of their number. As the concept became clearer, pulses jumped, for here was a firm tie-in with Cabeza de Vaca's story about the huge "cows" of the new land and of multistoried cities nearby.

Eager to learn more, Coronado prevailed on the amiable group to lead a party of his own men eastward to see Cicuyé and its surrounding lands—24 riders, four crossbowmen, Fray Juan de Padilla, and a lay brother, Luís de Ubeda. In high spirits they struck off through a malpais of congealed, jumbled, sharp-edged boulders of black lava that made the riders dismount and lead their suffering animals. This shortcut brought them to the amazing town of Acucu (today's Acoma), perched on the summit of a butte approachable (as far as the Spaniards saw) only by a stairway carved into the pink sandstone. After an uneasy confrontation at the base of the cliffs, the Indians of Acucu invited them to climb arduously to the top, where they were heaped with presents of hides, cotton cloth, turkeys and other foods.

Pleasant encounters characterized the rest of the journey east. Alvarado sent a cross ahead of his party

*The immense headland of El Morro, also known as Inscription Rock, was a landmark for western travelers. Lured by the shaded pool at the base, they camped nearby and often left a record of their passage in the rock's soft sandstone face. The party that Coronado dispatched to Acoma in August 1540 passed well south of the mesa and probably never saw it. The main army that ascended the Zuñi Valley several months later may have stopped at El Morro, but if so, they left no inscriptions. The headland is now the centerpiece of El Morro National Monument.*

# Acoma: Ancient Village in the Sky

Acoma embodies a thousand years of Pueblo life. According to an origin belief, the first dwellers were guided here by *latiku*, "mother of all Indians." Archeologists trace occupation to at least late Basketmaker times (AD 700). A few centuries later, ancestral Pueblos are living on top in houses of stone and adobe.

The native word for Acoma is ʔá·k'u, a word of ancient root that means "place of preparedness." In September 1540, Alvarado's men arrived at the great rock and marveled at the sight of the village and its people (about 200) on top. "The village was very strong," said a Spaniard, so difficult of access that no army could assault it.

The Acomans came down to the plain ready to fight the Spaniards. But when they saw that the intruders could not be frightened off, they offered peace and gave them

food and deerskins.
This illustration is artist
L. Kenneth Townsend's inter-
pretation of the village about
1540—a world outside time.

to the "province" of Tiguex (rendered Tiwa today), a concentration of 12 pueblos located on both sides of the Rio Grande in a broad valley at the foot of the abrupt Sandía Mountains. Thus prepared, retinues of important elders greeted them, decked out in ceremonial regalia and marching to the shrill piping of bone flutes. Presumably either Alvarado or Fray Padilla read them the *requerimiento* that made each town subject to the King of Spain. To this they added the Church's authority by erecting in the villages they visited, as far north as Braba (Taos), large crosses made by Brother Luís de Ubeda with an adze and chisel he had brought along for this purpose. Reactions were surprising, perhaps because the Indians also used varieties of the cross pattern in some of their ceremonies. They eagerly bedecked Brother Luís's Christian symbols with prayer feathers and rosettes made of plant fiber, sometimes climbing on each other's shoulders to reach the tops of the cruciforms.

Impressed by Tiguex's friendly people and stores of food, Alvarado sent Coronado a message suggesting that the recombined army winter there rather than in the high, cold lands of Cíbola. Then on he went across what is now called Glorieta Pass into the valley of the Pecos River.

There on a flat-topped ridge between a tributary stream and the main river was the finest pueblo the Spaniards had seen. The pattern was familiar: terraced houses rising four stories high around several plazas. Additional storage was provided in extensions running out from some of the corners of the main square. Balconies that provided walkways for the people on the upper floors served also to shade those beneath. Ladders running through holes in the walks served in the place of stairs. A constant need for firewood and building material had eliminated the forests for a mile or more around the pueblo, opening fine vistas of the high peaks of the Sangre de Cristo Mountains to the north, the red cliffs of Glorieta Mesa to the west, and the lower Tecolote foothills to the east.

By dominating the main trail linking the Plains Indians and the Pueblos of the Southwest, Cicuyé had become an even more powerful trade center than Háwikuh, and its people boasted that no enemy had been able to conquer them. But what of these bearded strangers who, with their swords and horses, had over-run Háwikuh in a single rush? Acting perhaps on the advice of Bigotes and Cacique, the people of Cicuyé decided to be friendly. An unarmed delegation marched out beating drums, playing on bone whistles, and carrying gifts. They listened blankly to the reading of the *requerimiento*, which demanded their submission to the King of Spain, then let the strangers rest among them for a few days (meanwhile keeping their young women out of sight), and gladly furnished guides when Alvarado announced he wished to continue far enough east to see the "cows" and the people who lived among them.

The guides were Plains Indians. Though they have been called "slaves" of Bigotes and Cacique, it seems more likely they were traders who, having been stranded in Cicuyé after bartering their goods, earned their keep by performing menial tasks while waiting for an opportunity to return home. One was named Ysopete, and may have been—accounts vary—the youth whose chest bore the tattoo of a buffalo. A Wichita Indian from central Kansas, Ysopete designated his homeland as Quivira: thus a new word in American mythology. With him was El Turco, the Turk, so-called by the Spaniards "because," wrote Pedro de Castañeda, "he looked like one." The resemblance probably arose from his turban, a headdress used by the Pawnees of eastern Kansas, or, in the Turk's language, Harahey.

*This ancient pueblo kiva at Pecos is one of two restored kivas in the park. At center is the firepit and stone draft deflector.*

Shortly after reaching the plains east of the Pecos River, Alvarado's explorers found themselves in the middle of a vast herd of buffalo. Lancing the huge beasts from a running horse and afterwards dining on the tender, roasted meat of their humps made for high living, but the sport was soon forgotten in a greater excitement. The Turk said he knew where there was gold. In Quivira. And even more in Harahey.

Did the Pawnee (if he was a Pawnee) really say that? Some anthropologists, Carroll Riley and Mildred Mott Wedell among them, have wondered. As a trader, the Turk knew a smattering of Nahuatl, as did the missionary friar, Juan de Padilla, one of his chief interrogators. To this stumbling *lingua franca*, El Turco added the fluent sign language of the Plains Indians, bits of which the Spaniards were beginning to pick up, though not as skillfully as they thought. Moreover, the talkers on both sides were discussing ideas and objects the others know nothing about. These opportunities for misunderstanding were immeasurably increased by the determination of Juan de Padilla to find the legendary Seven Cities of Antilia.

A word about Padilla. He had served as a soldier under Cortés in Mexico until deciding to enter the Franciscan order. He was hot-tempered, obstinate, and consumed with the hope of bringing the lost citizens—the wealthy, Christian citizens—of Antilia back into the mainstream of Catholicism. He believed implicitly that their gorgeous metropolises lay somewhere in the north. Meager Háwikuh and the Hopi villages had shocked him profoundly, but word of true urban centers farther east—Quivira!—reinvigorated his faith. He talked earnestly to the Turk about the kind of places he wanted to discover and listened with intense preconceptions to the trader's answers.

Out yonder, the Turk told him, was a wide river full of fish as big as horses. The canoes on the river held 20 or more rowers to a side, and their lords sat in the sterns under brilliant awnings. This tale corresponds with what the Gentleman of Elvas said about the canoes De Soto saw on reaching the Mississippi half a year later. So maybe El Turco had witnessed, during his wanderings, the Indian flotillas of the lower Mississippi and the fish as well—gar can reach 10 feet in length. The chiefs of the canoe tribes, he went on, were lulled to sleep by little bells of gold (*acochis*) tinkling in the breeze. They ate (a standard fantasy) from dishes molded out of *acochis*. But *acochis*, it developed years later, was a Spanish rendering of *hawichis*, a generic Pawnee term for any metal. Copper, perhaps? It was rare on the Plains and in the Southwest, but there was some and it was displayed conspicuously by important men.

That may be all the Turk said at first. But it was not all that Padilla and the rest of Alvarado's explorers heard. They harassed the Indian for proof that he was telling the truth. Frightened, eager to get them off his back, and desirous, possibly, of causing trouble for Bigotes, whom he may not have liked, El Turco said he had once owned a bit of *acochis*, but that Whiskers had taken it from him. The Spaniards understood that the object was a bracelet.

By then the autumn days were growing cold, and it was time for Alvarado to rejoin the army assembling in the Rio Grande Valley. On his way back through

Cicuyé, he confronted Bigotes and Cacique with El Turco's charge. They said they know nothing about the matter. Reluctant to set himself up as judge without Coronado's authorization, Alvarado seized the pair, put them in chains—as he later did the Turk and Ysopete when the one-time guides sought to disappear—and hurried out of the pueblo through a shower of curses and arrows hurled after him by the outraged inhabitants.

In Tiguex, too, affability had vanished. To provide shelter for the main army, which was moving eastward in sections, an advance group under hard-fisted Garcia López de Cárdenas had turned the people of Alcanfor pueblo out of their homes to find whatever refuge they could in neighboring towns. Coronado, who had taken a portion of the troops on a swing through the pueblos northwest of Tiguex, had just moved into the new quarters when Alvarado appeared with his captives. Immeasurably relieved by the thought that the costly expedition still might succeed, the general told Padilla, aflame with visions of the Seven Cities, and Alvarado to get the truth from Bigotes however they could. The inquisitors took him into a snowy field and set a war dog on him. Partly it was bluff; the victim was scarred but not disabled. Cacique, too, was attacked by a dog but less severely because of his age. Throughout the ordeal, which created deep resentment along the Rio Grande, both men persistently denied all knowledge of gold.

No dogs were set on the Turk. Though he, along with Ysopete, was also kept in chains so that he would be on hand when needed in the spring, his veracity was not questioned. For if the Turk was not believed, the expedition lost its meaning.

Until spring did arrive, survival was the goal. At first the Spaniards paid for the blankets, warm clothing, and food they requisitioned. Later, when the Indians, who had little surplus, held back, foraging parties roamed far and wide, taking what they desired without recompense, including in at least one case, a Puebloan's wife.

Sensing correctly that the horses were the Spaniards' main strength, the Indians struck at one part of the herd, killing two dozen or so animals and stampeding many others. Such attacks could portend disaster. With Coronado's blessing, Cárdenas stormed Arenal, the center of resistance. After breaching the

*Restored kiva of Kuaua pueblo, now preserved at Coronado State Park, Bernillilo, N.M. This village was long thought to be the Alcanfor pueblo that Cárdenas occupied. Though excavations in the 1930s failed to prove the speculation, the diggers did find these extraordinary kiva murals.*

79

walls with battering rams, the Europeans lighted smudge fires around the houses. As the gasping Indians fled into the open, making signs of peace, mounted horsemen struck down many. Others were tied to stakes and burned alive—a scene the Turk, Ysopete, and Bigotes were forced to watch so that they could tell the people of their villages what happened to rebels.

The episode occurred in December 1540. Shortly afterwards, the main part of the army appeared, worn out by forced marches through heavy snowstorms, but excited by rumors of gold, for the Turk, who by then knew more about the lusts of the invaders than they knew about him, was elaborating on his tales. With little to talk about but warm weather and wealth, the force lost its hold on reality and, like De Soto's, disintegrated into a kind of insensate organism responding only to the dynamics of survival. When a new center of resistance developed at a pueblo called Moho, the Spaniards burned the town after a long siege, killed many of the men who tried to flee, and made captives (as the *requerimiento* threatened) of more than a hundred women and children.

*Coronado's search for Quivira took him as far east as central Kansas. Fragments of chain mail armor found at several sites point to a Spanish presence in the 16th century. Coronado's men very likely saw country like this near Lindsborg, Kansas.*

Some ambiguity surrounds Coronado's part in these and other suppressions of "revolt." Though he was the army's commanding general, he apparently was never in the field during the moments of greatest carnage. He later testified he never authorized the burning of settlements or the use of dogs in battle. He personally took old Cacique back to Cicuyé and handed him over to his people, promising to release Bigotes as well when the army went through on its way to golden Quivira.

There was a practical side to the generosity, of course. He did not want a hostile fort astride his back trail when he made his final advance. Emphasize *final*. He badly needed a triumph to save himself from bankruptcy and to make the king's *audiencia* understand that what seemed atrocities had been necessary steps on the way to treasure for the empire.

The eastern advance began April 23, 1541. (Fifteen days later De Soto, heading west, sighted the Mississippi.) Bedlam marked much of the Spaniards' travel, especially during the daily making and breaking of camp. There were about 300 white soldiers, other hundreds of Mexican Indian allies, some with women and children, a herd of a thousand horses, 500 beef cattle, and 5,000 sheep—or so says Castañeda, possibly with exaggeration. The people of Cicuyé, seeing the mass advancing under a shroud of dust and remembering the fate of Arenal and Moho, became friendly again. They received Bigotes with rejoicing and heaped supplies on his one-time captors—anything to get the invaders moving on.

For many miles the Turk led the army east toward the Canadian River, along the path he had shown Alvarado. They saw so many buffalo—charging bulls killed a few horses—that Coronado would not venture guessing at the numbers. They fell in with a meticulously described, to the joy of future anthropologists, band of nomad Querechos, perhaps forerunners of the Apaches. As spring waned, they found themselves in the Texas Panhandle, atop the featureless immensity of the Llano Estacado, the Staked Plains.

At that point, the Turk, who the previous fall had told Alvarado that Quivira lay northeast, turned southeast. Why? Was he heading toward the lower Mississippi and the kind of civilization he thought the Spanish wanted? Or had he, during the pause in Cicuyé, agreed with the people there to lead the invaders into a trackless part of the plains where they would become lost and, deprived of maize, would starve.

Ysopete, who seems to have developed an acute antipathy for the Turk and who was anxious to reach his home in Kansas, warned Coronado he was being misled. Alvarado voiced suspicions. Coronado, however, clung to his necessary faith in the Turk until they reached a point where the abrupt eastern escarpment of the Staked Plains drops into almost impassable badlands. There at last he put the Turk in irons and turned the piloting over to Ysopete, assisted by some local Teyas Indians.

All this had taken precious time. To speed things along and to make food easier to procure, Coronado ordered the main army to return to Tiguex while he and 30 picked riders, 6 foot soldiers, Juan de Padilla, and a few mule packers scouted out Quivira.*

Traveling light and sparing their mounts, Coronado's group rode northeast for a month. They reached the River of Quivira (now the Arkansas) not far below present-day Dodge City, Kansas, and followed it, still

*Among the 30 riders was Juan de Zaldivar. As a consequence, Zaldivar had to leave behind a captive Indian woman he had picked up in Tiguex. Rather than return there she fled down a fork of the Brazos River that rises in the Staked Plains. Somewhere near present Waco, Texas, she perhaps met the surviviors of De Soto's party as they were trying to reach Pánuco, Mexico, by land. See page 50 above. If true, and it seems likely, it was the only contact between the two groups, who at one point were within 300 to 400 miles of each other.

northeast, to its Great Bend, where they left it. A little farther on they found the first Quivira (Wichita) village, a cluster of domed huts built of stout frameworks of logs overlaid with grass, so that they looked like haystacks. The surrounding land, rolling and fertile, produced fine corn, pumpkins, and tobacco. But no gold.

There were another 24 or so similar villages in the kingdom of Quivira. The Spaniards spent nearly a month riding disconsolately among them, gradually absorbing the truth that riches of the kind they wanted lay neither here nor, as far as they could learn, further east. (During the same period. De Soto was arriving at the same opinion while wandering through parts of Arkansas.) Angry questions were inevitable. Why had the Turk sought to mislead them both with his tales and his guidance? Under pressure he said the people of Cicuyé had put him up to it on the supposition he could lure the invaders to their doom. Perhaps they had. Or perhaps El Turco was simply trying, in his extremity, to shift blame.

The last straw came when Ysopete, El Turco's enemy, said the Pawnee was trying to stir up the Quivirans against the Spaniards. Acting on Coronado's orders, a party of executioners strangled and buried him, secretly at night lest the Quivirans be aroused.

There were no repercussions. Guided by several young Quivirans, the scouts returned by a direct route to the Rio Grande Valley, arriving in mid-September. In Coronado's mind, the absence of treasure was conclusive, but among those who had not gone to Quivira were many who believed that if the scouts had continued eastward, they would have found the Seven Cities. Coronado agreed half-heartedly to make another attempt the following spring, but fate intervened. During a horse race with a friend, his saddle girth broke and he was thrown under the hooves of his opponent's mount. Though his body gradually recovered, his spirits did not. After another miserable winter in Alcanfor, he ordered the army to start home. He was carried much of the way in a litter swung between two mules hitched in tandem.

By dying, De Soto escaped being tried for failure. Not Coronado. He was investigated for derelictions in connection with an Indian rebellion that swept his province immediately after his departure, for mistreating the Indians of Tiguex, and for failing to press

*On the great plains Coronado encountered a nomadic people he variously called "Teyas" and "Querechos." They were the buffalo-hunting Apaches, who followed the migrating herds, packing their goods from place to place on travois hauled by dogs. They impressed the Spaniards more than any Indians they had met. "They are a gentle people, not cruel," wrote the expedition's chronicler of the Apaches, "faithful in their friendship, and skilled in their use of sign."*

on beyond Quivira. Every enemy he had and a pack of opportunists and publicity hunters in quest of an audience took the stand against him, often blurting out scandalous rumors that had nothing to do with the case. Ill, his mind cloudy, he testified poorly in his own defense. But he had supporters, too, and in the end, largely through the help of Viceroy Mendoza, he was cleared of all legal charges. Though he lost the governorship of Nueva Galicia and some of his property there, he retained his seat on Mexico City's council until his health, poor since his return, broke completely. He died on September 22, 1554, aged 44.

There is a footnote. A few Mexican Indians stayed in Háwikuh and Cicuyé and a survivor or two were found in those towns when Spanish exploration of the Pueblo country resumed four decades later. Some religious people also stayed. One, old Fray Luís de Ubeda, the builder of crosses, settled at Cicuyé, hoping to spread Christianity by baptizing children. His fate is unknown.

Fray Juan de Padilla's tale is more dramatic. Obsessed with saving Indian souls by bringing them to the Church and dreaming still of the Seven Cities, he accompanied the young Quiviran guides back to their homes from the Rio Grande. Helping him drive along some pack mules, a horse, and a flock of sheep were two Indian *donados* of Mexico named Lucas and Sebastián, Andrés do Campo, a Portuguese, a black "interpreter," and a handful of servants. (Indians were not allowed to become full-fledged friars, but if they were "donated" to the Church by their parents, they could, as *donados*, serve as assistants.)

The missionary adventure was short-lived. While attempting to press on east of Quivira, the group was attacked by unidentified assailants. Padilla died, bristling with arrows. Do Campo, the two *donados*, and perhaps some others escaped. Separated, the *donados* and Do Campo traveled along different routes from tribe to tribe for at least four years until at last they reached Pánuco, Mexico—trips as astonishing but far less famed than the odyssey of Cabeza de Vaca, whose cross-continental traverse had put all these ill-fated land expeditions into motion. And so, except for the salt-water adventures of Juan Rodríguez Cabrillo, the epics had reached full circle.

# The Seafarers

History has preserved only dim outlines of the remarkable career of Juan Rodríguez Cabrillo, who died in 1543 while attempting to complete the first exploration of California's coastline. Though he is generally supposed to have been Portuguese, the evidence is too scanty to be sure.* There is no firm agreement about the cause or place of his death. He is variously reported to have used two, three, and even four vessels on his great exploration. Even his name has invited speculation. It appears on the few surviving documents he signed in the abbreviated form *Juan Rodz.* (The Portuguese spelling would normally end in "s," the Spanish in "z") What then of *Cabrillo*, which means "little goat"? Was it an affectionate nickname that he liked and used informally to distinguish himself from numerous other Juan Rodríguezes, a name as common in Hispanic countries as John Smith is in English-speaking regions? In any event he should be known formally as Juan Rodríguez. The name Cabrillo is, however, so firmly fixed in California history that it will be used in this account.

Whatever his name and origin, Juan Rodríguez Cabrillo learned seafaring in his youth. He arrived in Cuba in the second decade of the 1500s, perhaps as a sailor or, because of his age, as a page. Yet he apparently joined the Narváez expedition that was dispatched from Cuba to arrest Cortés as a crossbowman. Like most of his companions, he deserted Narváez and joined Cortés at Vera Cruz and afterwards survived the grisly *noche triste* when the Aztecs drove the Spaniards from their capital at Tenochtitlán. Immediately thereafter his chance came to display his nautical skills.

Cortés knew that if he were to recapture lake-bound Tenochtitlán, he would have to control the causeways that linked the city to the mainland. That meant building enough small brigantines to overpower the Aztec war canoes that had harried the retreating

*Too few records have survived for anyone to say with certainty where Cabrillo was born or grew up. Antonio de Herrera y Tordesillas, a Spanish chronicler, identified him in 1615 as Portuguese. Set against this is the testimony of the explorer's grandson in 1617 that "My paternal grandfather, Juan Rodríguez Cabrillo came [to the New World] from the Kingdoms of Spain. . . ." The NPS has adopted the view that Cabrillo was Portuguese. Many historians, including Cabrillo's most recent biographer Harry Kelsey, aver that he was Spanish. David Lavender believes that the question is both elusive and unimportant. What is certain, Lavender points out, is that like many adventurers from other countries Cabrillo spent a good part of his life in the service of Spain and opened new lands to Spanish settlement. *Ed.*

Spaniards so mercilessly during the *noche triste*. According to the soldier-historian Bernal Díaz del Castillo, Cortés put Cabrillo in charge of four "men of the sea" who understood how to make pine tar for caulking ships. But was that all the younger warrior did? Seamen were needed in all phases of the operation, beginning with the prefabrication of thirteen brigantines 50 miles from the capital and then transporting the pieces on the backs of at least 8,000 porters to the shores of the lake, where they were reassembled.

Each brigantine was manned by a dozen oarsmen, who also handled the sails. Each carried several crossbowmen and arquebus marksmen. The little fleet was important enough that Cortés took charge in person. A fortuitous wind enabled the brigantines to hoist sails and smash with devastating effect into a massed gathering of Aztec canoes. Afterwards they fought a dozen fierce skirmishes while protecting the footmen on the causeway — opportunity enough for a good sailor and fighter to catch the general's eye, if indeed Cabrillo was in the fleet, as he well may have been.

Tenochtitlán regained, the actual conquest of Mexico began. Small bands of Spaniards, reinforced by numerous Indian allies, radiated out in all directions. It is known that Cabrillo participated as an officer of crossbowmen in the conquest of Oaxaca. Later he joined red-bearded Pedro de Alvarado, cousin of Coronado's officer, Hernando de Alvarado, in seizing Guatemala and El Salvador. During those long, sanguinary campaigns Cabrillo performed well enough that he was rewarded with *encomiendas* in both Guatemala and Honduras.

An *encomienda* was a grant of land embracing one or more Indian villages. In exchange for protecting the village and teaching the inhabitants to become Christian subjects of the king, the *encomendero* was entitled to exact taxes and labor from them. Most grant holders ignored duties while concentrating on the privileges. What kind of master Cabrillo was does not appear. Anyway, for the next 15 years his Indian laborers grew food for slaves he had put to work in placer mines on his lands and in the shipyards he supervised on Guatemala's Pacific coast. He traded profitably with Peru and meanwhile enriched his personal life by taking an Indian woman as his consort.

With her he fathered several children. Later he brought a Spanish wife—Beatriz Sánchez de Ortega— into his extensive and, for the time and place, luxurious household.

Successful shipbuilding helped keep the excitement of the conquistadors high, for if the world was as small as generally believed, China, the islands of Indonesia, and the Philippines, discovered by Magellan in 1521, could not be far away. There might be other islands as well, ruled by potentates as rich as Moctezuma or inhabited by gorgeous black Amazons who allowed men to visit them only on certain occasions and afterwards slew them. There was that mythical "terrestrial paradise" called California in a popular romance of the time, *Las Sergas de Esplandián*. According to the author, seductive California was ruled by dazzling queen Calafia, whose female warriors wielded swords of gold, there being no other metal in the land, and used man-eating griffins as beasts of burden. What a spot to find!

The ships charged with searching for these places were built of materials hauled overland (except for timber) from the Atlantic to the Pacific by Indian bearers. The vessels were small, ill-designed, cranky, and often did not have decks. Nevertheless, ships sent out into the unknown by Cortés during the early 1530s discovered a strip of coast the sailors believed was part of an island. They were the first, probably, to refer to it as California, perhaps in derision since the desolate area was so totally different from the paradise described in the romance. The notion of nearby Gardens of Eden persisted, however, and interest soared again when Cabeza de Vaca's party reached Mexico in 1536 with tales of great cities in the north.

Cortés, who considered himself the legitimate *adelantado* of the north, tried to cut in on Mendoza's plans to exploit the Vaca discoveries. Rebuffed, he defied the viceroy by dispatching three ships under a kinsman, Francisco de Ulloa—one of the vessels soon foundered—to search for a sea opening to the lands of Cíbola. Finding himself locked in a gulf, Ulloa retreated along the eastern edge of the 800-mile-long peninsula that we call Baja California, rounded its tip and continued north to within 130 miles or so of the present U.S.-Mexico border. No inlets. His ships battered by adverse winds and his men wracked by scurvy, he returned to Mexico, only to be murdered, it is said, by one of his sailors.

The only man remaining who could have saved Cortés's dimming star was his old captain, Pedro de Alvarado, then governor of Guatemala. Dreaming of still more wealth in the sea, Alvarado, too, had built a pair of shipyards on the Pacific coast and had put Juan Rodríguez Cabrillo in charge of creating vessels out of materials dragged overland by Indians from the Atlantic. In 1538 Alvarado went to Spain and returned with 300 volunteers and a license to conquer any islands he found in the South Seas. By then he commanded 13 vessels, several of which had been built by Cabrillo. In the fleet were three galleons of 200 tons each, one of which, the *San Salvador* was owned and piloted by Cabrillo; seven ships of 100 tons, and three lesser brigantines. If Alvarado had thrown in with Cortés . . . but prudence dictated that he consult first with Mendoza, who had already invested some money in the building of the armada. So he took the fleet north to the port of Colima, due west of Mexico City and left it at anchor there, under Cabrillo's watchful eye, while he went inland to dicker with the viceroy.

In the end Mendoza and Alvarado agreed to share equally in the expenses and profits of a double venture: they would send some ships west to the Philippines and some north to Cíbola and then on to a strait called Anian, which supposedly sliced through the upper latitudes of the continent. The arrangements, which ignored Cortés's claims, sent the aging conquistador hurrying to Spain in 1540 in search of justice, as he defined justice. He never returned.

Alvarado had no opportunity to exploit the newly opened field. When an Indian revolt broke out in provinces of Jalisco and Michacán, the viceroy called on Alvarado to bring in his volunteers as reinforcements. During an engagement in the summer of 1541, a horse lost its footing on a steep hillside, rolled down and crushed Alvarado to death.

Onerous problems followed. Alvarado's estate had to be put in order; ships had to be refitted; the chaos of an earthquake at Santiago, Guatemala, headquarters of Cabrillo's holdings, had to be confronted. In due time Mendoza acquired control of the fleet, including the use of Cabrillo's *San Salvador*, and in 1542 launched the major explorations previously

*Navigation was still in its infancy in Cabrillo's day. Mariners sailed by "dead" reckoning, a method of figuring location by multiplying time by estimated speed over a given course. The main instruments were the compass, the hourglass, and the astrolabe. None of these devices was exact, and charts and mathematical tables were often inaccurate. Hence mariners sailed as much by instinct as by science. Skill often meant the difference between a successful voyage and wreck.*

agreed on. Ruy Lopéz de Villalobos took ships to the Philippines. On June 27 of that same year Cabrillo headed north with three vessels: *San Salvador*, which he captained; *Victoria*, commanded by pilot Bartolomé Ferrer (a pilot ranked just below a captain and was far more than a mere guide); and *San Miguel*, a small brigantine used as a launch and service vessel. It was commanded by Antonio Correa, an experienced shipmaster. More than 200 persons were crowded aboard the three vessels.*

Because both Ulloa and Alarcón had reported that the Sea of Cortés was a gulf, Cabrillo made no effort to follow the mainland north, but led his ships directly toward the tip of the peninsula, calling it California without comment, as though the name was already in current use. For nearly three months they sailed along Baja's outer coast, bordered much of the way by "high, naked, and rugged mountains." Because they were looking for a river entrance to the interior and for a strait leading to the Atlantic, they sailed as close to land as they dared, constantly tacking in order to defeat the contrary winds and the Pacific's erratic currents.

About August 20 they passed the most northerly point (Punta del Engaño) reached by Ulloa. A little farther on, where the land was flat, they beached the vessels to make some necessary repairs and, while exploring the neighborhood, found a camp of Indian fishermen. The native leaders, their bodies decorated with slashes of white paint, came on board, looked over the sailors and soldiers and indicated "they had seen other men like them who had beards and had brought dogs, *ballestas* [crossbows] and swords." Since there was no mention of horses, the strangers probably had come from ships. Ulloa's men of 1539? Hernando de Alarcón's of 1540? Or a later party, for there had been talk of Alarcón's returning for another venture inland. Mystified, Cabrillo entrusted the Indians with a letter for the bearded ones.

They relaunched the ships and another month dragged by—crosswinds, headwinds, calms. Cabrillo took constant sightings of sun and stars with his massive astrolabe, no small task for he had to stand with his back braced against a mast for steadiness on the heaving deck while he called out the readings that were to be recorded in the log. Speed was computed by throwing a wooden float over the stern and count-

*Recent scholarship has shown that accounts which say Cabrillo commanded two ships on his northern journey, as most accounts do, were following mistakes made by the first Spanish historians of the expedition. Unfortunately, Cabrillo's own log has disappeared and is known only through an often vague, chronologically mixed-up summary attributed to a Juan Paéz, of whom little is known. Better sources are the testimony given by witnesses in legal actions brought by Cabrillo's heirs to recover property taken from his estate after his death. For details see Harry Kelsey's biography, *Juan Rodriguez Cabrillo* (1986), and the Cabrillo Historical Association's 1982 publication, *The Cabrillo Era and His Voyage of Discovery*, especially articles by Kelsey and James R. Moriarty, III.

## *San Salvador*, Cabrillo's Flagship

Cabrillo himself built the ship he sailed up the California coast. It was constructed between 1536 and 1540 at Iztapa on the west coast of Guatemala. This region was something of a shipbuilding center, with a reputation for better quality than the yards of Seville, Spain. Much of the labor was furnished by Indians and black slaves, whole villages of whom were conscripted to portage supplies, raise food, cut lumber, trim timbers, and make pitch, rope, and charcoal.

*San Salvador* was a full-rigged galleon, with an approximate length of 100 feet, a beam of 25 feet, and a draft of 10 feet. The crew numbered about 60: 4 officers, 25 to 30 seamen, and 2 or 3 apprentices, and two dozen or so slaves, blacks and Indians. On the voyage to California, *San Salvador* also carried about 25 soldiers and at least one priest. The ship was armed with several cannon.

Ship's fare was wine, hard bread, beans, salt meat, fish, and anything fresh picked up along the way, all washed down by mugs of wine. Officers, who probably brought along food of their own and servants to prepare it, ate better. Slaves lived off rations of soup and bread and scraps left by others.

This illustration by John Batchelor is based on the research of Melbourne Smith.

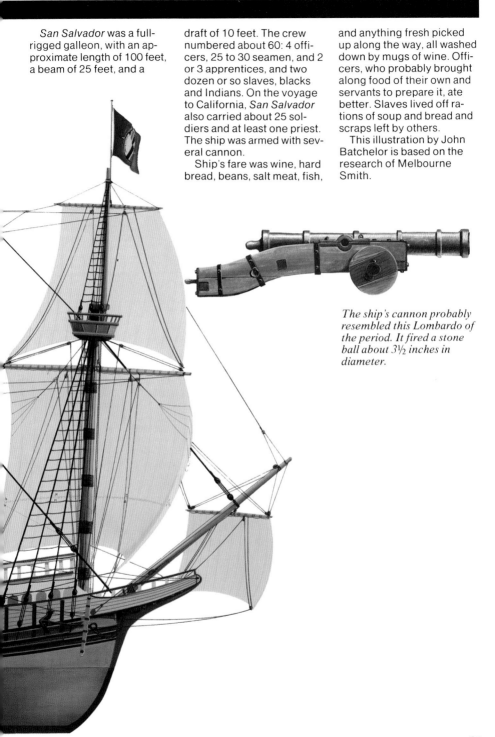

*The ship's cannon probably resembled this Lombardo of the period. It fired a stone ball about 3½ inches in diameter.*

91

ing the marks flashing by as the line holding it unwound from its reel. Compasses were used, but magnetic declinations were not well understood. All of Cabrillo's longitudes and latitudes were wide of the mark, but the fault was not entirely his or his instruments. He began his reckonings at a point inaccurately observed by others. Even the precise location of Mexico City was unknown in 1542.

On September 28, three months after leaving Mexico, the ships crossed the future international border and put into a "very good enclosed port, to which they gave the name San Miguel." It was our San Diego.

The Indians there were afraid. That evening they wounded, with arrows, three men of a fishing party. Instead of marching forth in retaliation, Cabrillo sailed slowly on into the harbor, caught two boys, gave them presents, and let them go. The kindness worked. The next day three large men partly dressed in furs (the "Summary" says) came to the ship and galloped around to illustrate horsemen killing Indians far inland. Melchior Díaz, fighting Yumans during his crossing of the Colorado in the fall of 1540? Or had word of Coronado's battles at Háwikuh and on the Rio Grande trickled this far west along the trade trails? In any event, Europeans were no longer a mystery. On three more occasions Cabrillo picked up rumors of Spaniards in the interior.

After easily riding out the first storm of the season in the harbor, the ships sailed on, pausing at Avalon on Santa Catalina Island and later at the island we call San Clemente. Along the way they remarked on the many flat-lying streamers of smoke from Indian villages near San Pedro and, later, Santa Monica Bays (warnings, unrecognizable then, of temperature inversions and smog). Somewhere near modern Oxnard, they spent a few pleasant days with Chumash Indians, admiring their big, conical huts and their marvelous plank canoes. Tantalized by a fresh rumor of Spaniards near a large river (the Colorado?), Cabrillo sent out a letter in care of some Indians "on a chance." But where the river reached the coast, if it did, he could not learn.

The coast from Oxnard to Cabo de Galera (our Point Conception) runs roughly east and west for nearly a hundred miles before bending sharply north. This stretch was heavily populated. Many canoes traveled alongside the ships, and there was a great

*A deadeye and a triple-purchase block of the type used on San Salvador. Deadeyes and lanyards were employed in fixed rigging, frequently to secure shrouds that supported the mast; opposite is a typical setup, by which lines were tightened and secured to the vessel's frame. A block and tackle were essential for hoisting heavy yards. Drawings by John Batchelor.*

deal of calling back and forth and exchanges of gifts. A string of islands, also populated, paralleled the shore, forming what is now called the Santa Barbara Channel. On October 18 the Spanish ships endeavored to round Cabo de Galera but were blown by strong winds out to the westernmost of the Channel Islands, one the mariners had not yet explored. They named it Posesión (it is now San Miguel) and remained in the shelter of Cuyler's Harbor for about a week.

The idyllic days were over—and so, in many critical ways, is agreement between Juan Páez's "Summary" of Cabrillo's log and the testimony about the trip given in 1560 to the *audiencia* of Guatemala by Lázaro de Cárdenas and Francisco de Vargas, both of whom told the court they had been on the trip.

During the stay on Posesión, according to the "Summary," Cabrillo fell and broke his arm near the shoulder. In spite of that, he resumed the journey, rounded Point Conception, was again driven back, tried once more, and in mid-November succeeded. The fleet soon reached the rugged Santa Lucia Range, in which William Randolph Hearst four centuries later built fabulous San Simeon. For the mariners it was a heart-stopping area—"mountains which seem to reach the heavens. . . . Sailing close to the land, it appears as though they would fall on the ships. They are covered with snow."

They may have sailed as far as the vicinity of Point Reyes, a little north of San Francisco Bay, or they may have gone no farther than Monterey Bay, where they almost certainly anchored on November 16. Whatever their northernmost point, they turned back, probably because of bad weather, possibly because of Cabrillo's sufferings. On November 23 they once again landed on San Miguel Island. There, sensing he was about to die, Cabrillo made the pilot, Bartolomé Ferrer (or Ferrelo in some accounts) swear to continue the explorations. On January 3, 1543, he perished and was buried on the island.

Or was he? In 1901, an amateur archeologist, Philip M. Jones, found on Santa Rosa Island, just east of San Miguel, an old Indian *mano*, or grinding stone, into one of whose sides a cross and the fused initials JR had been incised. The stone was stored in a basement at the University of California, Berkeley, until 1972, when Berkeley's noted anthropologist, Dr. Robert Heizer, began wondering whether the curiosity

The Indians that Cabrillo encountered along the Santa Barbara coast were the village-dwelling Chumash. Their villages were groupings of houses, according to a later traveler, with a sweat-house, storerooms, a ceremonial plaza, a gaming area, and a cemetery some distance off. The houses were cone-shaped, spacious and comfortable. A hole in the roof admitted light and vented smoke from cook fires. Apart from the brief skirmish at San Diego Bay, Cabrillo found the California Indians a gentle, friendly people.

*Two views of the Chumash: Above is an early illustration of two fishermen, from George Shelvocke's* Voyage Around the World, *1726. At right, is artist Louis S. Glanzman's drawing of a woman with a garment. "They were dressed in skins," said Cabrillo's diarist, "and wore their hair very long and tied up with long strings interwoven with the hair . . . attached to the strings were many gewgaws of flint, bone, and wood."*

*This stone found on Santa Rosa Island may have once marked the burial place of Cabrillo.*

might have once marked Juan Rodríguez's grave. So far extensive examinations have determined nothing about this additional mystery.

And then there is the testimony of Cárdenas and Vargas in 1560. They said, without giving dates, that Cabrillo decided to winter on Posesión, which the witnesses called La Capitana, and that on stepping ashore from the ship's boats he fell between some rocks, broke his shin bone, and died 12 days later. Vargas adds that the fall resulted from Cabrillo's hurry to help some of his men, who were battling Indians. A splintered shin bone with its possibilities for gangrene sounds more deadly than a broken arm.

On February 18, 1543, after beating around the Santa Barbara Channel for more than a month, exploring and taking on wood and water, Ferrer resumed the trip, as Cabrillo had asked. Standing well out to sea, he scudded north until on March 1 he was opposite—who knows? Cape Mendocino? The California-Oregon border? The mouth of the Rogue River? Wherever they were, the sea, breaking over the little ships with terrifying fury, was driving them irresistibly toward the rock-punctuated shore. They prayed fervently, and suddenly the wind shifted, driving them south "with a sea so high they became crazed." The storm separated the ships, *San Salvador* ran out of food, and the sailors were in dire straits until they were able to land at Ventura and later San Diego, where, in addition to food, they also picked up a half a dozen Indian boys to train as interpreters in case of a repeat journey.

Miraculously, the ships rejoined at Cedros Island off Baja California, and on April 14, 1543, they reached Navidad, nine and a half months after their departure. There was no repeat journey. Like De Soto and Coronado, they had located neither treasure nor shortcuts to the Orient. After that, no one else wanted to try, and Spain's first great era of exploration of the United States came to an end.

# Epilogue

Judged on the basis of what they set out to do, De Soto, Coronado, and Cabrillo failed. Yet great consequences flowed from their efforts. Without intending it, they found truth. They exploded myths and gave a solid anchor to the Spanish imagination. Undistracted, the people of New Spain could settle down to developing the resources—the mines, plantations, and ranches—that lay close at hand. It was the perceived need to protect this new wealth from potential enemies in the north—France, England, and Russia—and not the frenetic hope of riches that eventually brought about the extension of the Spanish empire into what became the southern United States, from St. Augustine, Florida, to the Franciscan missions of California.

Another discovery was the tremendous size and geographical diversity of America north of Mexico. After the truth had trickled out about the forests and savannahs of the semi-tropical southeast, the vast deserts and striking headlands of the southwest, the spreading central plains with their immeasurable herds of buffalo, and the coastal mountains and misty valleys of California, no one would ever again think of the upper part of the continent as a mere bulb perched on the thin stem of Central America and Mexico. These vast stretches, moreover, were peopled by a race never before known. By bringing back the first sound anthropological descriptions of these people, the Spanish explorers—and the French and English after them—gave the philosophers of Europe new food for speculation concerning the human condition.

Most important, they, along with the explorers of other nations, brought a sense of release and fresh possibilities to the Old World. Their reports arrived at a time when custom-bound Europe was struggling to shake off the constraints of ancient traditions, outworn feudal institutions, and an almost total lack of specie for implementing the quickening trade of the Renaissance—an average of less than $2 in currency for each of the continent's 100 million people. In the Americas there were no mossy customs, but there were precious minerals and raw materials beyond imagination awaiting development. Development by anyone with daring and ingenuity. The great *conquistadores* had all arrived poor and unknown and then had discovered within themselves explosive energies for meeting unprecedented physical challenges. Such strengths, once they were turned from brigandage into constructive endeavors, became the hallmark of the new continent. Pointing the way were Cabeza de Vaca, De Soto, Coronado, and Cabrillo, all doing their great work within a decade. It is indeed an era to remember.

---

*Mission churches were the vanguard of Spanish civilization in the Southwest. They softened the imperatives of the state and eased inexorable cultural transitions. San Jose Mission was established along the San Antonio River in 1720. Still an active parish, the mission today is a unit of San Antonio National Historical Park, Texas.*

# A Guide to Sites

# Following the Explorers

Though nothing spectacular survives, travelers can find many rewarding historical places that conjure up the Spanish *conquistadores* and the natives they encountered. The four principal NPS sites are described briefly in the following pages. Many other parks and several Indian communities also preserve landscapes directly associated with the explorations. They are listed below. All these places are well worth a visit and several are worth a journey to anyone interested in the beginnings of North American history.

| | |
|---|---|
| **Ocmulgee National Monument**<br>**Macon, GA 31201** | Ancient mounds built by people of the Mississippian culture. De Soto passed through this region in 1540. |
| **Etowah Indian Mounds State Historic Site**<br>**Cartersville, GA 30120** | De Soto visited this town (called Itaba) in August 1540. |
| **Mound State Monument**<br>**Moundville, AL 35474** | A farming town which flourished AD 1000-1500; representative of the powerful chiefdoms found by De Soto. |
| **Parkin Archeological State Park**<br>**Parkin, AR 72373** | Believed to be a center of an important chiefdom (Casqui) visited by De Soto in 1541. |
| **Coronado State Monument**<br>**P.O. Box 95**<br>**Bernalillo, NM 87004** | A Pueblo village visited by the Coronado expedition in 1540. Polychrome murals in the kiva are a prize exhibit. |
| **Pueblo of Acoma**<br>**P.O. Box 309**<br>**New Mexico 87034** | A fortress town inhabited by descendents of the Pueblo people who befriended the Alvarado party in 1540. |
| **Zuni Pueblo**<br>**Box 339**<br>**Zuni, NM 87327** | The original Cíbola of Spanish legend. Háwikuh, the place of Coronado's first encounter with Pueblo Indians, is now a ruin. |

De Soto National Memorial commemorates the first major European penetration of the southeastern United States. De Soto's purpose, sanctioned by the King, was to conquer the land Spaniards called *La Florida* and settle it for Spain. He failed in both objects. There was no rich empire in the north, only a succession of chiefdoms, and his practice of looting villages and grabbing hostages alienated native inhabitants and turned his march into a siege. The lasting significance of the expedition was the information it yielded about the land and its Mississippian people in a late stage of that remarkable civilization.

The park was established in 1949 on the south shore of Tampa Bay. De Soto's fleet may very well have sailed

by this point in May 1539 to a landing spot farther around the bay. Attractions at the park include replicas of the type of weapons carried by the expedition and thickets of red mangrove, the so-called Florida land-builder. The journals tell of De Soto's men cutting their way inland through mangrove tangles.

For more information about the park and its programs, write:
Superintendent
De Soto National Memorial
P.O. Box 15390
Bradenton, FL 34280

*Demonstrations in winter give insight into military life and the Spanish world-view in the 16th century. De Soto's army may well have come ashore at a spot on Tampa Bay that resembled this beach within the park (far left). Below: replica armor and an early marker commemorating De Soto's bold march.*

Following an ancient Indian trade path up the San Pedro valley, the Coronado expedition crossed the present Mexico-United States border just east of this park. Hikers on the Coronado Peak Trail looking down Montezuma Canyon can see in the far distance cottonwood trees that mark Coronado's line of march.

The national memorial was established in 1941, 400th anniversary of the expedition. Its setting high in the Huachuca Mountains is a fitting place to recall the first major Spanish *entrada* into the American Southwest in all its color and fire: the gathering of the army at Compostela, arduous marches across wilderness, encounters with native cultures of great sublety and art, discovery of a land of vast expanse and

power, and above all the record of where they had been and what they had seen.

This is a park to see on foot. Trails lead to good viewing points and connect with others in Coronado National Forest, which surrounds the park.

For information about the park and its programs, write Superintendent Coronado National Memorial 4104 E. Montezuma Canyon Road, Hereford AZ 85615

*The Huachucas rise like islands above the surrounding Sonoran desert. This landscape is little changed from Coronado's day. The expedition traveled along the San Pedro River, east of the park.*

The ruins of Pecos Pueblo and Spanish missions of the 17th- and 18th-centuries crown a small ridge overlooking the Pecos Valley in upper New Mexico. At the time of the Coronado *entrada*, the pueblo was a giant apartment house, several stories high, with a central plaza, 600 rooms, and many kivas—home to 2,000 souls. The village prospered because it commanded the trade path between Pueblo farmers of the Rio Grande and buffalo hunters of the Plains. Pecos was a crossroads of commerce and culture, and its people grew adept at trade and war. The arrival of Franciscan priests in the 1600s with Spanish custom, religion, law inexorably altered Pueblo life. The Spaniards built a spacious mission church on the south end of the ridge, and

Pecos
National
Historical
Park

*The kiva and the mission church frame the two worlds of the Pecos Indians. During the Pueblo Revolt of 1680, Pecos Indians destroyed the first mission and built this kiva (now restored) within the mission's convento. For a few years they followed their religion undisturbed. Right: Extensive pinyon-juniper forests once surrounded Pecos Pueblo. The vessel is a 16th-century olla, the Spanish spur dates from the 17th century.*

a second but smaller one when the first church was destroyed in the Pueblo revolt of 1680. Pecos continued as a mission for more than a century. Disease and Commanche raids spelt decline in the late 18th century. The last inhabitants—fewer than 20—drifted away in 1838.

The park is 25 miles southeast of Santa Fe. Among its features are the ruins of the ancient pueblo, two restored kivas, and adobe mission walls. For information on the park and its programs, write:

Superintendent
Pecos National Historical Park
P.O. Drawer 418
Pecos NM 87552-0418

This park honors the man who led the first European exploring expedition along the California coast. Sailing under a Spanish flag, Juan Rodriguez Cabrillo departed on 27 June 1542 from the port of Navidad on Mexico's west coast. He commanded the ship *San Salvador* (with a crew of a 60); with him was *Victoria*, and another smaller vessel. His objective: "to discover the coast of New Spain." Three months later he hove to in "a very good enclosed port"—San Diego Bay. This was the mariner's first landfall north of Baja peninsula. Cabrillo himself died and was buried in the Channel Islands. His crew went on to explore as far north as Oregon, seeing new landmarks and new peoples, not all friendly.

The park is located on

*The Old Point Loma Light-house, built 1854.*

Point Loma, within the city of San Diego. Features include a heroic statue of Cabrillo, dramatic views of the Pacific and San Diego Bay, and Old Point Loma Lighthouse, a 1850s structure. In winter, the point is a good place to see the annual migration of the gray whale.

For information about the park and its programs, write:
Superintendent
Cabrillo National Memorial
P.O. Box 6670
San Diego CA 92166

Cabrillo
National Monument

*Gray whale migrations in winter are an annual spectacle.*

*The 14-foot sandstone statue of Cabrillo is the work of Portuguese sculptor Alvaro DeBree. Completed in 1939 for the San Francisco World's Fair, it was eventually relocated here. The portrait is conjectural; there is no known likeness of the explorer.*

# Essay on Sources

If any of the leading *conquistadores* who march through these pages kept a running account of his adventures, the journal has been lost. Except for occasional letters, the closest we can come to firsthand information are reminiscences written or dictated by lesser participants many years after the events described. Some supplementary material also comes from court testimony. More immediacy is lost by the fact that most English readers must depend on translations of varying accuracy and fluency. There are several translations of all main documents.

The first of the New World adventurers to reminisce in print was Cabeza de Vaca. His *Relación . . .* appeared in 1542. Buckingham Smith's English translation, first printed in 1855, was later included with several other documents in *Spanish Explorers in the Southern United States, 1528-1543,* edited by Frederick Hodge and Theodore Lewis (New York, 1907).

The same work also contains Smith's translation of *Narratives of the Career of Hernando de Soto* by an anonymous Hidalgo (gentleman or knight) of Elvas, Portugal, first published in Portugal in 1557 by a survivor of the long march. Smith's translation, somewhat modified, reappeared in Gaylord Bourne's two-volume *Narratives of the Career of Hernando de Soto* (New York, 1904). Bourne's volumes also contain reminiscences by Rodrigo Ranjel, De Soto's secretary, and Luis de Biedma, the latter a spare account. The longest and lushest of the De Soto tales is *The Florida of the Inca,* the Inca being Garcilaso de la Vega, son of a Spanish father and an Incan mother. He drew his information from the oral accounts of three of De Soto's soldiers and used his active imagination to embellish what he heard. The first complete English translation, by John and Jeannette Varner, appeared in 1951 (reprinted by University of Texas Press, 1980). Miguel Albornez has published a novelized biography, *Hernando de Soto, Knight of the Americas*, translated by Bruce Boeglin (New York, 1986).

Some secondary material, which uses anthropological, archeological, and geographic research to shed light on the early explorations, should be mentioned. One instance: *Final Report of the United States De Soto Commission*, John R. Swanton, chairman (Washington, D.C., 1939). The commission sought to retrace De Soto's zigzagging route. Jeffery P. Brain's new edition of the *Final Report* for the Smithsonian Press (Washington, D.C., 1985) revises Swanton's conclusions in many places. Another interesting formulation is "De Soto Trail: National Historic Trail Study, Draft Report" (NPS, 1990). In an appendix Charles Hudson offers a new reconstruction of De Soto's route. The articles in *First Encounters: Spanish Explorations in the Caribbean and the United States, 1492-1570*, Jerald T. Milanich and Susan Milanich, eds., (Gainesville, 1989), fill out our understanding of New World societies during the first decades of exploration.

Still the best introduction to Coronado and his expedition is Herbert E. Bolton's classic biography, *Coronado: Knight of Pueblos and Plains* (1949). George P. Hammond and Agapito Rey have brought together in *Narratives of the Coronado Expedition* (Albuquerque, 1940) all the primary documents, including testimony from Coronado's trial, that anyone except specialists needs to know about the first Spanish *entrada* into the American Southwest. The chief items are the *Relacións* of Juan de Jaramillo and Pedro de Castañeda. Castañeda's *Relación* also appears in Hodges and Lewis.

A sampling of the historical dispute over Friar Marcos's doings in the Southwest can be found in articles by Henry Wagner and Carl Sauer in the *New Mexico Historical Review*, April 1937, July 1937, and July 1941. See also Cleve Hallenbeck, *The Journey of Fray Marcos de Niza* (Dallas 1949). The place of the religious in the Coronado expedition is examined by Fr. Angelico Chavez of New Mexico in *Coronado's Friars* (Academy of American Franciscan History, Washington, D.C., 1968). John L. Kessell's *Kiva, Cross, and Crown* (National Park Service, Washington, D.C., 1979) looks at the relationships between the Coronado expedition and the key pueblo of Pecos. Albert H. Schroeder has analyzed Coronado's route across the Plains in *Plains Anthropologist*, February 1962. Carroll L. Riley, in the *New Mexico Historical Review*, October 1971, and *The Kiva*, winter 1975, shows that in Coronado's time long trade routes and hence a rudimentary system of verbal communications, fortified by signs, linked Cíbola (Háwikuh) and the Indians of Mexico. Other trade trails carried goods and knowledge from the interior across the Colorado River to the Pacific and out onto the Plains. A new account of Coronado's march is Stewart L. Udall, *To the Inland Empire* (New York, 1987).

The principal sources on Cabrillo (Juan Paez's "Summary Log" and court testimony about Cabrillo's accomplishments) were published by the Cabrillo Historical Association in *The Cabrillo Era and His Voyage of Discovery* (San Diego, 1982). The best biography, Harry Kelsey's *Juan Rodriguez Cabrillo* (The Huntington Library, 1986), is based on extensive new research in sources.

☆GPO:1992—312-246/40005

# National Park Service